W9-CZU-125

DEVELOPMENTAL PSYCHOMETRICS

DEVELOPMENTAL PSYCHOMETRICS

A Resource Book for Mental Health Workers and Educators

By

JACK L. FADELY, Ed.D.

Associate Professor of Special Education and Educational Psychology
College of Education
Butler University
Indianapolis, Indiana

and

VIRGINIA N. HOSLER, M.S.

Diagnostic Learning Center
Peoria Public Schools
Peoria, Illinois

CHARLES C THOMAS • PUBLISHER
Springfield • Illinois • U.S.A.

Published and Distributed Throughout the World by

CHARLES C THOMAS • PUBLISHER
Bannerstone House
301-327 East Lawrence Avenue, Springfield, Illinois, U.S.A.

This book is protected by copyright. No part of it may be produced in any manner without written permission from the publisher.

© 1980, by CHARLES C THOMAS • PUBLISHER
ISBN 0-398-04056-7 cloth
ISBN 0-398-04057-5 paper
Library of Congress Catalog Card Number: 79-28746

With THOMAS BOOKS careful attention is given to all details of manufacturing and design. It is the Publisher's desire to present books that are satisfactory as to their physical qualities and artistic possibilities and appropriate for their particular use. THOMAS BOOKS will be true to those laws of quality that assure a good name and good will.

Library of Congress Cataloging in Publication Data

Fadely, Jack L 1934-
Developmental psychometrics.

Bibliography: p.
Includes index.
1. Psychological tests for children. 2. Educational tests and measurements. I. Hosler, Virginia N., 1943- joint author. II. Title. [DNLM: 1. Psychometrics. 2. Child development. BF39 F144d]
BF722.F32   370.15′028′7   79-28746
ISBN 0-398-04056-7
ISBN 0-398-04057-5 pbk.

FLORIDA GULF COAST
UNIVERSITY LIBRARY

Printed in the United States of America
C-1

PREFACE

IN RECENT YEARS there has been a significant increase and diversification of mental health services within the community as opposed to the traditional institutionalized programs for children with behavioral disorders. The term *behavioral disorders,* in fact, has come to represent the general services available for children who display emotional and social disorders in the school and community. Furthermore, the general concept of community mental health services has broadened to include learning, as well as developmental, difficulties that children often experience as a consequence of or an instigator of emotional and social difficulties. Such difficulties as neurotic or psychotic syndromes of deviance in behavior have, with increased sophistication in child development and increased understanding of neurological functioning, become less receptive to the traditional diagnosis of psychological and psychiatric methodology.

The present treatment of emotional and social difficulties includes a differential and team-based diagnosis that reflects a greater understanding of the myriad of factors affecting behavior. The more traditional personality diagnosis focused primarily upon the etiology of emotional and intrafamily factors as the primary cause of emotional difficulties. Such a diagnosis often focused only on problematic behavior and often missed those areas of behavior which reflected positive and adaptive skills of the child. Areas of nutrition, cultural background, perceptual motor abilities, language development, and learning difficulties are now included as important aspects of understanding both the assets and liabilities of the child.

With the increasing diversification of services and professionals involved with children who display behavioral disorders, efficiency and cost have become major problems in providing services. The solitary diagnostician who also provided the bulk of treatment services is becoming less common. Today's diagnostic services often include psychologists, social workers, psychiatrists, behavioral clinicians, recreational and educational therapists, and nursing personnel. This range of professionals is often required in order to fully understand the child's behavior and his needs. It is becoming more common to find diagnostic and treatment personnel who are not psychologists or psychiatrists but rather who are personnel with varying degrees and training, including educators and nonclinical mental health workers. Under the supervision of a psychologist, the nonclinical personnel are providing more input during the diagnostic stage in many cases. Thus, in some mental health centers and school programs there may be several professionals such as social workers, psychometrists, counselors, and teachers who may be involved in both diagnosis and treatment of children with behavioral disorders. This means that much of the diagnosis is pressed down toward the "front line" on intervention as opposed to the traditional psychological or psychiatric level of assessment.

The authors have found in recent years an increasing number of professionals in education, psychology, and mental health who have entered master's level programs looking for some means of increasing their own diagnostic skills at the nonclinical level. This is a broad range of personnel, and yet, their needs are essentially the same. The purpose of such training, for these personnel, is to gain some means of providing a screening program in which a broad range of developmental and behavioral factors can be assessed without the need for a complete psychological and psychiatric examination. In many cases this front line assessment not only is an adjunctive and supportive program of clinical diagnosis, it actually supplants it.

The present book is designed for mental health, medical, and educational personnel who must do front line screening and diagnosis of children with behavioral disorders. The material in the book provides an overview of a comprehensive screening process that can be accomplished at the front line level of assessment. A major purpose of the book is to assist the reader in recognizing the need to assess both positive and negative aspects of the child's behavior and to assess the implications of this process for treatment. While the book provides the general structure and much specific material that can be used in diagnosis, it relies on the reader to obtain additional materials that will provide a comprehensive observational and objective assessment. If the reader intends to develop adequate diagnostic skills, then it is very important to purchase recommended materials. With the additional materials and the guidelines in the book, nonclinical personnel can develop diagnostic skills that are in many ways commensurate with those of the psychologist. Another major intention of the book is to provide the means whereby diagnostic skills at the front line level of assessment can provide practical information that can immediately be translated into treatment objectives. In more difficult cases the information will provide significant assistance to clinical personnel who may later do more in-depth assessment. Clarification should be made here concerning the term *nonclinical* personnel. The word nonclinical refers to personnel below the M.D. and Ph.D. level of training and not personnel who should be considered clinicians. This distinction is important, for certified psychologists are able to give tests that are more sensitive than nonclinical personnel can give. Yet, the nonclinical personnel can usually, with the proper instruments and training, provide diagnostic information that is commensurate with much that is obtained in clinical testing. This reality provides the means for more efficient diagnostic services so that every child will not have to be seen for in-depth clinical examinations.

The authors wish to thank Kit Applegate for her assistance in editing the text as well as Carol Zindel for her help in typing the final manuscript.

J.L.F.
V.N.H.

CONTENTS

DEVELOPMENTAL PSYCHOMETRICS

Chapter 1

GENERAL LEVELS OF DEVELOPMENTAL ASSESSMENT

I N RECENT YEARS there has been an increasing amount of information produced relative to the evaluation of child and adolescent development. The earlier concepts of development such as intelligence, nature-nurture controversies, basic notions of personality, retardation, and social effects of cultural deprivation have all come under study within professions that serve the needs of children and adolescents. Many of the more trusted notions about child behavior have been altered not only by psychologists and educators but also by neurologists, anthropologists, child development specialists, sociologists, and a host of other professionals who have added great amounts of information and research on the nature of learning and behavior. It is no longer possible to simply blame the child's culture, his intelligence, or his genetic heritage for his many difficulties or, for that matter, to credit his assets to one or even two specific internal or external factors. The fields of linguistics and computer theory (cybernetics) have added significant changes to our notions of how the human mind functions and learns. The systems concept of information processing and the more intricate assessments of interrelated psychological and sociological factors operating within the human mind have brought to the fore a much more expanded awareness of behavior.

Educational principles are dramatically changing the way the behavior of children is assessed and the consequences of that assessment. This development of newer concepts of assessment is valuable to all mental health professionals, a collective phrase that will be used to include school counselors, behavioral clinicians, social workers, nursing professionals, and teachers. The following principles have set the stage for such assessment being accomplished by those other than psychologists, psychiatrists, and those traditionally regarded as having primary rights to the assessment of behavior and learning.

1. Behavior is a complex system of learned responses occurring as a consequence of the interaction of the integral parts of the central nervous system, opportunities for learning in the environment, and open-ended but semi-structured experiences provided by the individual's tutor.

The fixed concept of intelligence has given way to the realization that intelligence is not a thing but rather the consequence of a variety of interdependent variables that are multidimensional rather than linear. The child does not simply begin life with a predetermined basis of behavioral competencies; rather, given a set of certain neurological probabilities, the result of experience and opportunity can either increase or decrease eventual behavioral competency. Intelligence is merely a statistical means of measuring the growth of a child relative to certain expectations at any point in time. Intelligence, then, is a ratio of developmental efficiency in learning.

Specific behaviors of a child that are ineffective, within varying limits, can be changed through educational intervention. The number of potential ways in which the efficiency of child learning and behavior can be changed is limitless and depends as much on the intervention of the teacher as the capacities of the child.

The belief in a multidimensional concept of behavior requires a more sophisticated means of assessment than merely giving a test to determine adequacy of learning. Further, these tests often are biased and yield data that more likely fit the beliefs of the examiner than the limits of a child's behavioral potential. Merely giving tests is not enough. There has to be a more comprehensive means of establishing the competencies of the child.

2. Development has to be assessed through a broad range of factors including both positive and negative aspects of behavior, which can show the multidimensional characteristics of the child's behavior.

Too often, tests are given to find out what is wrong with a child, resulting in a diagnosis of a disorder or disability rather than being given as a comprehensive means of establishing the general nature of the child. The authors have participated in many school and clinic diagnostic conferences concerning a child's problem in which the primary concern was how to solve the "problem" rather than to determine comprehensive competencies of the child. Assessment should include at least certain factors that give as comprehensive an overview of the child as possible, including not only deficit areas but positive aspects of the child as well. Major areas of behavioral competency include perceptual and motor development, language development, general learning skills, social and cultural aspects of behavior, and personality. Within each of these areas are many subcategories, but these general areas must be included. In many cases diagnosticians concern themselves only with the area of difficulty that is their specialty.

In recent years there has been an increasing need to have diagnostic teams seeing children, because one individual cannot provide the expertise to assess a wide range of abilities. This has greatly increased the cost of assessment and in many ways made it less effective due to the conflicting opinions of various professionals among themselves.

3. Differentiation of assessment levels must be developed so that every child does not have to be given expensive and time-consuming assessments outside of the classroom or clinic in which the intervention or treatment is to occur.

As assessment has become more complex its administration has tended to move further away from the actual point of intervention. This means that the teacher tends to be less involved in the actual assessment; as a consequence, she often places less value on the assessment along with having difficulty in understanding or applying the treatment. It has also been our experience that the farther away from the point of intervention the assessment occurs, the less likely it will be to have accuracy for the intervention. Another difficulty is that much intervention involves "killing flies with a shotgun," for many problems could be resolved at a more basic level than in the psychologist's or psychiatrist's office if the means for making such assessment were available to the front-line practitioner.

If ten children present behavioral problems, learning problems, or some sort of psychological difficulty, it is the authors' experience that at least six to eight of those children can be assessed on the front line rather than giving all of them some sort of complete battery of tests by several professionals. More assessments should be carried out by front-line personnel (level 1), rather than by a limited number of professionals as consultants to the basic team (level 2), or (level 3) by a team of professional diagnosticians. By equipping all mental health professionals with the means of completing front-line assessments, several advantages would be derived. Children who do not need extensive assessment could be given an evaluation on the spot where intervention is to occur. In this way less cost would be involved. Constant reassessment could be accomplished as the program proceeds with immediate alteration in the program, and only children requiring highly sophisticated assessment would take up the time of the professional diagnostician.

It is the intent of this book to provide, for the teacher and mental health professional, skills that at the present time are not an inherent aspect of their practice or training. These skills are what the authors term collectively *developmental psychometrics,* which at the present time are being offered to only a limited number of professionals. Developmental psychometrics involves assessment procedures for treatment within the classroom or clinic and can be used as a basis for interface functions with outside agencies and the home.

Developmental psychometrics includes the following areas of professional skills:

1. Assessment of cognitive and intellectual abilities of children and adolescents.
2. Assessment of perceptual-motor abilities and skills of preschool, elementary-school-aged and secondary-school-aged children.
3. Assessment of social and personality skills of school-aged children.
4. Parent counseling as related to the foregoing areas of concern.
5. School and community interface functions related to the recognition of the need for assistance for such difficulties.

The development of developmental psychometrics, measurement of the psyche, essentially means the assessment of various aspects of development having to do with learning, perceptual-motor skills, learning abilities, intelligence, and general personality and social skills. It is not the intent of this book that the mental health professional will supplant those services normally provided by psychologists, psychiatrists, and social workers. The case is quite the contrary. It is the intent that the mental health professional will be able to provide a valuable screening program as a member of an interdisciplinary team that begins in the classroom and may involve referrals to any of several professional or service agencies. This is why the term *psychometrics* is used. It indicates that the process is a special one whereby various screening measures and instruments are used at the "front line" of interface between the child's family and the treatment and services field. More in-depth assessment can then be undertaken within a specific specialty area if needed.

Specifically, the following information can be made available to other professionals on the team providing services and making treatment decisions. This information can also be used as referral data to pinpoint more specifically the nature of the services required by an outside agency.

1. Developmental age levels in
   a. Gross motor skills
   b. Fine motor skills
   c. Visual-perceptual skills
   d. Language skills — verbal skills
   e. Intellectual assessment — cognitive skills
   f. Basic reading levels in word recognition and reading comprehension
   g. Writing skills
   h. Specific memory recall
   i. Sequential memory recall
   j. Social skills
   k. Personality skills
2. These data will assist in diagnosing
   a. Learning difficulties and learning disabilities
   b. Verbal expressive disorders

   c. Dyslexia
   d. Developmental hyperactivity
   e. Mental retardation
   f. Family communication difficulties
   g. Dysgraphia
   h. Emotional disorders

These screening data will provide the team with specific information that can be evaluated and recommendations then made either for assistance within the school setting or referral for in-depth testing and/or treatment by other social and health-care professionals.

In our work with teachers and health- and social-care professionals it has been found that nonclinical tests available in developmental areas can provide the same information as clinical tests, the only difference being that the level of training required to give the tests is not as difficult and the information is more practical. In a large number of cases, this level 1 testing done by the teacher yields enough definitive information so that treatment can be provided without further referral. This avoids referral of children to additional costly and time-consuming services that are not always needed. It does make referrals more accurate and give definitive information upon which to make needed referrals. In this manner, only those cases requiring professional psychological or psychiatric assistance are referred. This is one of the positive aspects of this level of assessment. If the disposition of the case does require referral for additional evaluation or treatment, the data provided should be useful to the following resources:

1. Psychiatric services
2. Psychological services
3. Specialized pediatric services
4. Neurological services
5. Educational programs and services
6. Counseling and social services

The assessment data provided by the psychometrics will assist in interdisciplinary communication and provide more effective interschool services.

An immediate question that the teacher or mental health professional may ask is, how much time will this sort of assessment require? The amount of time will depend upon the nature of the assessment, what purpose the assessment is to serve, and whether outside agencies are involved or will be involved, requiring additional communication time, report writing, and parental counseling. The following are some of the logical strategies that will be used in the psychometric services.

1. Language and intellectual assessment — 20 to 30 minutes
2. Gross and fine motor assessment — 15 to 20 minutes
3. Visual perceptual and vision screening — 5 to 10 minutes.
4. Learning skills — 10 to 15 minutes
5. Social-personality assessment — 30 to 60 minutes, variable

Language and Intellectual Assessment

Assessment of language and intellectual skills may be accomplished with children when there is some question of their overall developmental competency. It is often quite important to know the exact rate at which the child is developing so that any difficulties can be assessed and appropriate recommendations made to the parents and school. Language assessment does not include a speech or audiological assessment. Some professionals, knowledgeable about language development, assume that this area includes a speech and hearing assessment. Articulation and audiological examinations may be indicated, but the tests discussed here deal primarily with psychological and neurological aspects of development, as opposed to language assessment, which involves a significantly different investigation.

Language development involves the use of expressive cognitive skills, the understanding, synthesis, and expression of language, and is therefore quite apart from the articulation and audiological factors. While disorders in speech and hearing may affect speech production, a child can develop adequate language skills. Thus, the language assessment is the measurement of what language is known and how it is used.

Because the central role of language is communication and verbal skills, it is the primary mode of determining intelligence in most schools. In recent years nonverbal skills have come under study, and we now know that they too are an integral part of intelligence. Language development and language skills continue, however, to be the most accepted modalities in relation to both formal learning and intellectual functioning. It is for this reason that the teacher should be able to assess these skills.

Gross and Fine Motor Assessment

Gross and fine motor development are areas of development that include evaluation of various motoric functions in relation to central nervous system function and potential neurological difficulties developmentally. However, in the assessment procedure, while some indications of neurological difficulties may show up during the evaluation, the primary goal is to assess general motoric development in relation to learning and various developmental processes, which can affect more formalized learning. For example, the psychometrics assessment is concerned with the child's general motoric skills in relation to such things as left-right organization, spatial relationships, and the comprehension of forms and symbols related to learning to read. In this way it is not the clinical assessment of neurologically related function but whether behavioral skills are developing.

Visual-Perceptual and Vision Screening

Children who experience various fine and gross motor difficulties often exhibit difficulty in using the eyes effectively to track words on a page, to correct their movements through visual analysis during writing exercises, and to maintain visual fixation and fusion over the periods of time required for formal learning. These difficulties are not vision problems in themselves but are more related to the general lack of gross and fine motor function that the eye muscles demonstrate, and other more generalized motor difficulties.

Learning Skills

General learning skills can be evaluated with some degree of ease, and this greatly aids the team in relating various difficulties developmentally to specific learning problems. Again, as in the case of several other areas of assessment, the learning skill evaluation is not one of great depth but rather a survey of general skills. This can greatly improve communication between educators and other personnel when the child's needs are discussed.

Social-Personality Assessment

Aside from the many potential inferences about personality that can be obtained during the general assessment, there are also many nonclinical devices and approaches that can be used with the parents to ascertain the difficulties of a child's social and personality development. These areas are much more variable and less easily evaluated than the foregoing, but a survey of such skills is an important aspect of the overall evaluation. Often, while completing an assessment of learning skills or other developmental abilities, the evaluator will recognize the need for gaining information that relates to personality and social skills.

These areas constitute the essential concerns of this book. The discussions will allow the professional to obtain the basic skills of psychometric evaluation in relation to services. Many materials are provided within the text, but it obviously is redundant to attempt to produce testing materials when many excellent ones are already available. The book provides the basic text and directions, but to become competent in using psychometric skills the reader will have to purchase a minimum number of diagnostic instruments once the program is to be initiated. Local psychologists and school psychologists available in most communities can assist the professional should specific questions arise in the use of the tests. However, this text along with the recommended tests should be adequate for the professional to "go it alone" in a self-taught and text-guided program. The battery of tests should be purchased and used with this text during the time when staff persons are learning the concepts. There are usually many relatives or friends who are willing to allow their children to be used for practice, and before attempting to administer a test to a patient the practitioner should practice and become familiar with the administration of the instrument or approach.

Chapter 2

INTELLIGENCE, DEVELOPMENT, AND LEARNING

THERE IS A DISTINCT difference between what is commonly considered intelligence by most parents and that which is known by psychologists and social theorists. Intelligence is a global concept that is largely a statistical and normative theory. Intelligence, as a developmental behavior or characteristic of specific animal species including the human being, has been a concept that has caused much suffering and confusion within professional groups. It does not exist as a single variable that can be measured by any known instrument, and its interpretation varies so much that it is nearly impossible for even the professional to clearly define it. The medical practitioner has often been as much if not more confused than those professionals in fields such as education and psychology concerning exactly what "intelligence" involves. Intelligence is much like the concept of life. In recent years the medical profession has begun to wrestle with the difficult decision of when an individual is truly to be pronounced deceased if he is still physiologically functional though mentally inactive. Medically, such questions as biological death versus brain death, or the differentiation between central nervous system function and general body function have become critical problems in treatment. The body may "live" without the normal function of the brain through the "machinery" now available to sustain the body systems long after central nervous system response in the form of consciousness has ceased to exist. The central issue is, when may a person be said to be dead, or, stated positively, what is the definition of the actual state of life? Intelligence, like life, is a relative term that refers to a variety of human behaviors. Intelligence, as such, does not explain or define the complicated set of behaviors that may be viewed as intelligence.

Intelligence, then, is a general term that implies some sort of

12

specific behavioral set, which does not, in fact, define that be-havior in an objective manner. First, let us describe some of the common beliefs about intelligence and then discuss how such concepts might be used in the clinic in a useful way.

1. People who can talk well are intelligent.
2. Intelligence is inherited from your parents.
3. People with college degrees are intelligent.
4. You have to go to school to be intelligent, or only intel-ligent people can pass in school.
5. Boys are more intelligent than girls.
6. Adults are more intelligent than children.
7. Unskilled laborers are not intelligent.
8. Certain animals are more intelligent than others.
9. Scientists are intelligent.
10. Lower-class people are less intelligent than middle- or upper-class people.

Many of these statements appear somewhat silly, yet a large number of parents often communicate these beliefs to their children. For example, there is a definite tendency for much of the population to believe that those people who make a lot of money are "smarter" than those who make less. The inference is, of course, that one must be intelligent to make a lot of money. Even though most people who are interviewed on the street would not agree with the above statements, their general be-havioral patterns do reflect these beliefs.

While these statements are often seen as somewhat "unin-formed" by professionals in various fields, every professional field reflects some sort of bias about intelligence and social class — the concept of the "average" person, the idea that individuals who have higher levels of education are brighter, and even that athletes are less intelligent. The obvious characteristic of each of these beliefs is that they reflect a cultural, social class, and monetary-value system that operates to correlate "success" with something called intelligence.

How does one evaluate and measure intelligence? Not so long ago it was not unusual to hear college professors in education and psychology tell their students that intelligence was what intelligence tests measured. This idea may seem absurd, but it is still not uncommon, even today. Before discussing the nature of intelligence and the problems associated with its measurement, we will look at some behaviors that appear to indicate the presence of intelligence. This is only a partial list, but it will help us begin to narrow in toward a workable definition for the mental health professional.

Intelligence involves —

1. The ability to adapt behavior, which allows the individual to adjust or act in ways consistent with the environment within which he lives;
2. The ability to learn cultural-specific responses to activity in the environment around him;
3. The ability to learn and classify specific perceptual characteristics of the environment;
4. The ability to use abstract symbols, i.e. words and numbers, to represent actual experiences;
5. The ability to manipulate in abstract form, to experience and direct responses toward performing a new behavior in a unique situation that has not been practiced;
6. The ability, based on past experience (memory), to predict certain probabilities of activity in the present environment;
7. The ability to recall, when needed, specific experiences and symbols that will assist in understanding a present situation;
8. The ability to abstract a concept of self and to view that abstraction in relation to present, past, or future situations;
9. The ability to create transformations of ideas internally, resulting in novel and unique ideas;
10. The ability to comprehend potential meaning beyond present reality, such as in religious beliefs.

This list is somewhat esoteric, but it provides a general orientation to the difficult aspect of so-called intelligent behavior. When the biologist speaks of "intelligent" behavior in insects, or the anthropologist speaks of intelligent behavior in primitive man, the use of the word *intelligence* implies quite a different viewpoint than is the case in the concept of modern man. There is a vast difference between what the intelligent child does and what the scientist finds of interest in lower animal or insect behaviors. Thus, the word *intelligence* has far-ranging and varied meanings depending upon the context within which it is being used. When we study the behavior of children, the notion of intelligence most often refers to some sort of adaptive behavior that is related to both developmental-neurological aspects of behavior and the interaction of the potential with the environment. One cannot infer that because a child does not act intelligently, he is in fact unintelligent. Our problem of defining intelligence in children has both quantitative and qualitative inference, and both of these dimensions must be evaluated in reference to a specific value system of expectations that are socially and culturally defined.

All of this leads to the statement of fact that when a child's behavior is evaluated on some scale of intelligence, the evaluator must be very careful how and when such inference is made. The most stable reference of intelligence is that of some sort of ratio that describes the child's behavior in relation to the behavior of other children relative to psychoneurological factors. For example, most children learn to walk independently at approximately twelve months. It could be said that a child who walks at the appropriate age is displaying a sort of motor intelligence appropriate for the average child. The child who begins to produce single words at about the age of nine to fourteen months is displaying appropriate language development and, therefore, might be said to have average language intelligence. Children who walk or talk early may be said to be brighter than other children, while those who develop late may be said to be less intelligent. These two examples are simplistic, yet they illustrate the basic notion of how intelligence is applied in education and psychology. In medical terms either child may be said to be displaying appropriate development.

Intelligence tests were originally developed based on the concept that certain abilities and skills appear in predictable fashion at certain times in a child's life. It was assumed that bright children tended to develop at a more rapid pace in a range of specific behaviors, while slow or retarded children not only developed more slowly but they often leveled off sooner, never reaching full maturity in many areas of development. The more retarded a child might be the slower his development and the sooner he tended to level off. In earlier years it was common for adults to describe a retarded adult as "having a mind of a four-year old" or some other designation. These descriptions were actually a means of describing the slower development and the eventual leveling off or plateauing of specific developmental abilities. Intelligence then came to be measured by observing the various areas of development of children and establishing average ages when certain abilities or skills seemed to naturally appear. In this fashion, intelligence was actually the measurement and establishment of a learning expectation ratio. A scale was developed in which an intelligence ratio was established with a 0 to 200 range with 100 being average. A 100 IQ means simply that the child is displaying average rates of development on a range of specific factors considered important to adaptive and learning behavior. This ratio was determined basically by dividing the child's mental age (MA) by his chronological age (CA) and multiplying by 100. While this is somewhat of an over-simplification, it serves to communicate the still-existent method of determining intelligence. For example, a child with a chronological age of ten who scores appropriately on an IQ test at the nine-year-old level would have an IQ of 90.

Intelligence tests have become much more sophisticated in recent years, and few professionals rely on the mental age-chronological age ratio. However, the basic concept still remains the general notion. Today the Wechsler Intelligence Scale for Children (WISC), the Wechsler Adult Intelligence Scale (WAIS), and the Wechsler Preschool and Primary Scale of Intelligence (WPPSI), although not true measures of intelligence, are the most widely used and respected measurements of intelligence. These tests are individually administered, allowing for observation of the behavior of the individual, and result in scaled scores that no longer rely on a MA/CA ratio but on a score derived from the more complicated variables of differences in ages of development. These three tests separate tasks into two major divisions — verbal tasks, and performance on sensory-motor tasks. This division provides the examiner with the differentiation between the child's abilities in verbal and nonverbal functions and allows for some cautious correlations of responses on the subtests and neurological functions in the various areas of the central nervous system. For example, individuals with neurological deficits in the left-hemisphere language functions often display various indications of difficulty on the verbal portions of these tests. Spatial-motor functions normally associated with the right-hemisphere functions appear to correlate well with the performance portions of the tests. Along with a neurological examination, often more subtle indicators of neurological specificity can also be derived from various subtests. Many of the older intelligence tests did not have a separate intelligence scale for nonverbal functions, and differential intelligence factors were either ignored or unknown. For psychologists and educators the awareness of these two major areas of intellectual function aids greatly in not only understanding the child's behavior but in providing for differential treatment of any intellectual difficulties that might be present.

There are several individually administered intelligence tests, but the WISC, WAIS, and the WPPSI continue to have the most widespread acceptance and use among psychologists. Although these tests require special training for optimum use and would not be practical for use by teachers, nurses, or social workers, it is important for them to understand the sorts of abilities that most individually administered tests measure. Such a passing understanding can assist the professional in gaining a clear concept of exactly what is inferred from intelligence testing. The verbal portion of the WISC intelligence test is divided into the following various subtests:

1. Information — Measures general information and knowledge.
2. Similarities — Measures the ability to verbally associate, classify, and form remote relationships.
3. Arithmetic — Measures mathematical concepts involved with language, i.e. as in story problems.

4. Vocabulary — Measures word knowledge and vocabulary.
5. Digit Span — Measures short-term auditory sequential memory.
6. Comprehension — Measures judgment and practical reasoning ability.

From the foregoing subtests certain key abilities appear important, and it will help the mental health professional to recognize what abilities are measured by psychologists and school personnel. It is apparent that these tests suggest that the following abilities are important to adequate intellectual functioning:

1. The ability to learn and retain certain facts about the environment in which the child lives and be able to report these on demand.
2. The ability to see relationships in verbal material. For example, how is an orange like a pear? This ability involves several mental functions including visualization of the objects, the ability to make mental comparisons, and the ability to group or classify objects and ideas.
3. The ability to grasp the relationship between mathematical symbols (numbers) and the actual material being added, subtracted, etc. The key is the ability to abstract concrete material through representation of the actual object.
4. The ability to learn words, to group them in meaningful phrases, and to recall such words and explain their meaning. This again involves *abstraction* of concrete objects and ideas and replacing them with words that represent them.
5. The ability to retain, organize, and repeat information in logical sequence. This involves both abstraction and sequential organization.
6. The ability to use information and values in making decisions that are appropriate to the situation in which the judgments are applied. This involves a synthesis of many of the foregoing abilities and involves primarily application and use of information.

Recent research has indicated that much of language function is lateralized into the left cerebral hemisphere. Though some language comprehension and vocabulary ability are available in the right hemisphere, the major synthesis of language functions occurs in the left hemisphere in normally developing human beings. There are many variations of this tendency, and brain damage in the left hemisphere at early stages of development can to some degree be resolved through lateralization of partial function in the right hemisphere. It is important to recognize that trauma and lesions to the left hemisphere can severely affect the foregoing verbal abilities, and as one might expect, the level of intellectual functioning could be impaired.

The performance portion of the WISC includes a number of subtests that purport to measure various aspects of nonverbal and spatial perceptual intelligence. The performance section of the WISC includes the following subtests:

1. Picture Completion — Measures the ability to visually identify details in common everyday objects and the ability to separate essential from nonessential visual details.
2. Picture Arrangement — Measures the ability to use visual motor function to fit parts into a whole, to think sequentially in visual areas, and to understand cause-effect relationships.
3. Block Design — Measures the nonverbal problem-solving ability, visual-motor coordination, and the ability to relate things spatially.
4. Object Assembly — Measures visual-motor coordination, the ability to fit parts into a whole, and spatial relationships.
5. Coding — Measures visual-motor coordination, manual dexterity, and flexibility.
6. Mazes — Measures planning and anticipation ability, and visual-motor coordination.

The first characteristic that one notes about these subtests is that there appears to be much overlap between the various tests. One problem is that when the test was created, much less was known about nonverbal intelligence than now. Nonverbal intelligence was still seen primarily as a function dealing with visual-motor coordination. It has been shown in recent years that nonverbal intelligence is as critical and complicated as verbal intelligence. It is now known that these nonverbal functions appear to be synthesized in the right hemisphere, and the WISC has become more useful in recognition of certain neurological difficulties in that hemisphere. Further, research is strongly suggesting that much of what is commonly described as intuition, creativity, and insight are functions of the right hemisphere. When integrated with language functions, the child is provided with a complementary set of computers, the right and left hemispheres, which can solve more complex problems than either alone.[1]

The foregoing subtests appear to measure more than just visual-motor coordination. The following is a list of probable intellectual factors involved in these subtests:

1. The ability to recognize and remember visual information as well as associated visual symbols and material both on a verbal and nonverbal basis, i.e. common objects and words in print.
2. The ability to systematically make a visual analysis according to some pattern of culturally learned behavior.
3. The ability to gain personal meaning from visual information.
4. The ability to visually comprehend behavior, and the use or function of objects and materials.
5. The ability to analyze the directional spatial orientation of forms and structure and the reasoning ability to organize spatial forms.
6. The ability to gestalt whole images from partial forms or fragments of a whole, depending upon visual abstractions and memory.
7. The ability to spatially sequence and organize information and to retain such images through visual memory for later reproduction.
8. The ability to make nonverbal decisions and solve problems.

From these test items, verbal and nonverbal, it can be seen that there are certain abilities and skills that are assumed to form the basis for intelligence. Yet, these tests do not measure intelligence directly, for it should be obvious that the actual basis for intelligence is the interaction between the environment (learning) and the integrity and maturity of the central nervous system (neurological functioning). If we were to attempt to measure intelligence directly it would finally become a physiological analysis. How well does the central nervous system function in relation to the tasks that are required in a particular culture? Obviously, when the intelligence test is used we are not measuring neurological function directly but rather we are inferring such function from the "learned" responses of the child. What is truly being measured, at best, is learning. This means that even with the best instruments available for measuring intelligence, the actual factors involved are not something called intelligence but learning. It is assumed that if a child learns certain expected behaviors, then he is more or less intelligent than most other children who were also given the test.

It is important to remember these concepts regarding the measurement of intelligence, since many parents, the general public, teachers, and even psychologists actually believe that intelligence tests measure intelligence. There is nothing wrong with this concept; in fact, it is quite useful because it provides a means of comparing developmental rates and learning skills of children. Regardless of its usability, intelligence is not the factor that intelligence tests measure. Intelligence is rather a matter of statistical and theoretical assumptions about human behavior and not a tangible or measurable entity within the human.

Why is it so important to make such a distinction between what is generally assumed to be intelligence, and what is more realistically simply a ratio between what a child learned and what he would be expected to have learned for his particular age? The most important overriding factor is that if we cannot actually measure intelligence and if what we call intelligence is actually a learning ratio, then this should change our concept about intelligence. For example, if we felt we were actually measuring intelligence and we found that a child's IQ was 85 then this would infer a capacity. If his intelligence were actually 85 then he would be a slow learner and we would not expect too much from him. We would teach him what we felt he could learn having an IQ of only

85. Conversely, if we understood that the intelligence score simply represented a ratio between what has been learned and what would be expected to be learned, then our approach is totally different. We do not know if the child is motivated, if the environment is conducive to learning, if the opportunity to learn in the most effective way is there, or if given extra time and assistance what the child might learn. In effect, if we think of intelligence in terms of a variable ratio, dependent upon opportunity and practice in learning, then we might, with the appropriate program, increase the child's intelligence. This is the contemporary way of looking at so-called intelligence. It is assumed that if the child is at least at the slow-learner level of functioning, the upper limits of performance may be difficult to determine if adequate educational intervention is provided. This is very different from the first case in which we limit opportunity because a child only has an IQ of 85.

It has long been known that many factors, other than lack of opportunity and practice, can affect the level of a child's functional abilities and skills. Children may exhibit delayed development due to maternal deprivation, child abuse, emotional difficulties, learning disabilities, visual or auditory deficits, and a host of other factors, including that they simply do not like the teacher or the examiner. All of these factors are open to change and resolution. Severe retardation is perhaps the only condition in which intervention may have no appreciable effect on increasing the child's abilities and skills to any significant degree. Beyond severe retardation, it is assumed that every child can, given the opportunity and practice, increase his ratio to some degree. As might be guessed, test validity and reliability on many intelligence tests are rather poor because of all of the variables that interact both in school and in the testing situation.

In recent years intensive work has begun on the development of newer forms of intelligence tests. However, they may not be called intelligence tests but simply measurements of relative developmental rates in specific areas that are easily identifiable and more related to known sequences of mental and physiological growth.

At present the mental health professionals who may use the material in this book need some means of objectively measuring intellectual functioning of children under their care. Because the WISC and the WPPSI are tests requiring special clinical training in psychology, other adequate tests should be available for the mental health professional that can give a good estimate of the intellectual functioning of the child at the screening level, though the clinical depth available to the professional in psychology will not be available. It has been the authors' experience that extensive screening procedures using a measure of intelligence within a battery of tests can give information that is adequate for office purposes.

Two tests, the Slossen Intelligence Test and the Peabody Picture Vocabulary Test, have been widely used by nonclinical personnel to gain an accurate measure of a child's intelligence. These two tests can be administered quickly, usually within five to ten minutes each, yielding an overall intelligence score that correlates well with that obtained by the psychologist on the WISC or WPPSI. Again, these are intended to be measures that are used within a battery of tests by the mental health professional for purposes of screening a child's developmental abilities. In most cases, the tests used in the batteries discussed in this book will provide the mental health professional all of the psychometric data needed to provide assistance for the child or to make the appropriate referrals or recommendations to the parents. We are not attempting to make clinical psychologists of nurses, teachers, or social workers but rather to provide them with the means of obtaining immediate information within their particular setting, which can assist the child and his parents in their needs.

For the mental health professional a complete involvement in intelligence testing is not, after all, the essential problem. It has been implied here that intelligence testing has two major benefits. It provides a score that illustrates a child's relative development in some area to that of other children of similar age, and it can assist in inferring specific developmental disabilities or problems that need attention. There are also the general needs of the mental health professional who has a child with some sort of behavioral or learning difficulty. While two intelligence tests are included in the screening batteries suggested in this book, additional areas of concern will also be screened. While a general developmental score of verbal competence will be helpful, the IQ test is, after all, too often a measure of language development. Beyond the intelligence tests the mental health professional should screen language development more directly, so as to observe specific areas of problematic behavior. Further, the mental health professional needs more than a score such as that given on the WISC for spatial motor development. Thus, in the screening battery there needs to be some means of looking at spatial motor development. As can be seen, our concern is not for scores of intelligence but rather a more comprehensive battery of tests that measures all of the following factors: cognitive and intellectual abilities, perceptual motor skills, social and personality skills, learning skills, and indicators of specific developmental difficulties. Intelligence tests have too often provided the only general measurement of development, and in recent years knowledgeable professionals have come to realize that it is specific developmental abilities that must be given for analysis and not some esoteric concept of intelligence. How well the child develops language, perceptual motor skills, social and personality skills, and how well he learns are all specific areas of development that make up the so-called "intelligent behavior" deemed so important on intelligence tests. It does not help the mental health professional to know that a child has a score of 85 on an intelligence test. What he has to know is why is that so and what are the specific areas of development that need stimulation. How can he assist the parents? How can they assist their child? How can the school assist the child? These questions cannot be answered by a score. One must know the factors present that prevent normal functioning.

In our work with children, certain factors appear most prevalent in determining developmental rates of children. These are factors other than the obvious medically related ones such as mental retardation or insults to the central nervous system through prenatal or birth difficulties, falls, accidents, or disease. They include the following:

1. An inability of parents to know how and when to provide specific learning opportunities for infants and children.

2. Specific intrafamily difficulties that affect the care of a child, such as divorce, poor marital relationships resulting in child neglect or abuse, immature parents who provide inadequate nurturing and care, and maternal deprivation.
3. Parenting problems dealing with siblings and providing inadequate attention and care for each child, such as in large families where parents are inadequate as providers and supervisors of children.
4. Families where the father does not take an active role in child care and management, leaving this to the mother.
5. Highly mobile families where the children receive inconsistent learning opportunities and care.
6. Unrealistic expectations of parents for their children, resulting in stress and anxiety in the children.
7. The tendency of parents to expect the school, the physician, and other agencies to provide care and assistance for children rather than the parents providing it themselves.
8. Neurotic parents who provide highly protective environments for their children where they are unable to explore and develop naturally.
9. Inadequate educational programming for children with special needs.
10. A lack of involvement by the parents in their child's school and community experiences.

Aside from the usual medical problems, it is for these difficulties that it is hoped this volume will provide some assistance to the mental health professional. The adult who understands developmental difficulties and the needs of children is the key to learning and development for the child with problems. In the following chapters, general guidelines are provided for the mental health professional who wishes to develop skills in developmental psychometrics.

It is assumed that individuals who will use this book will purchase the needed materials. These involve several tests that will compose a battery of screening instruments along with the materials provided in this book. At the outset, the individual wishing to develop psychometric skills should order the listed materials in each section.

References

1. Spradlin, W. W. and Porterfield, P. B.: *Human Biology From Cell to Culture.* Hiedelberg Science Library, Springer-Verlag, pp. 29-30, 1979.

Test References

1. *Slossen Intelligence Test*
   Slossen Educational Publications
   140 Pine St.
   East Aurora, New York 14052
2. *Peabody Picture Vocabulary Test*
   American Guidance Service
   Publishers Building
   Circle Pines, Minnesota 55014

Chapter 3

THE SCHOOL-COMMUNITY INTERFACE

THE RELATIONSHIP between the child's school, home environment, and the outside agencies has traditionally been one that has been tenuous at best and nonexistent at worst. There has been somewhat of a distinct separation between services provided and the needs of children in relation to learning and community environment.

As the role of the specific developmental factors has come to be understood more and more by parents, the mental health professional has been approached more frequently to evaluate and interpret specific developmental difficulties that might affect learning and behavior. As the area of child development continues to grow, the relationship between the mental health professional and the community will also grow. This is not always a welcome relationship, since most mental health professionals already find it difficult to keep abreast of educational developments. Again, this difficulty and new expectations from school and community have stimulated the creation of the present volume. It is hoped that this book can provide a useful form of information and interface skills that can lighten and make more effective this increasingly important relationship between the community and the school.

The mental health professional has been traditionally involved in certain behavioral-developmental problems that interfaced with learning, such as severe mental retardation, physical disabilities, and many genetic and disease-oriented disorders that require special educational intervention. In recent years, however, several specific developmental difficulties have come under educational supervision, requiring a closer relationship even when the traditional problems do not exist. These developmental difficulties include the following:

1. Delayed development and slow-learning children who were not diagnosed as mentally retarded but displayed

27

some sort of neurologically related problem that delayed or inhibited learning;

2. Learning disabilities including minimal brain dysfunction, hyperactivity, and dyslexia;
3. Cultural deprivation and related physical and emotional disabilities;
4. Difficulties in attention span, behavioral organization, concentration, and emotional difficulties.

These four areas of concern may be classified as developmental delays, learning disabilities, behavioral organization difficulties, and emotional problems. These classifications are of special interest in that they exist only because of new information. Less than twenty years ago none of these difficulties were even recognized by educational professionals. There have always been children who display significant neurological difficulties. There have always been children who were considered subnormal intellectually, and there have always been children with severe emotional difficulties.

The identification of these special areas of difficulty in learning is the result of both improved educational and psychological knowledge about how children learn, and increased specificity in child development and medical aspects of human behavior. Twenty years ago, unless a child was blatantly mentally retarded or physiologically handicapped, difficulties in learning were assumed to be emotional or temperamental. As our knowledge in human behavior has increased, we have come to realize that there are a number of subtle but sometimes surprising developmental conditions that can decrease learning disabilities. Medical knowledge about neurological development and disorders, and increased understanding of how developmental factors affect learning, have brought the educator and psychologist to the door of the medical clinic for assistance. It is a wedding that science instigated, and however unwilling any of the participants, it appears the marriage will continue.

In the early years of this marriage many significant problems have arisen, and much social and medical controversy has occurred both within the educational field and the practice of medicine. We are still feeling our way and attempting to deal with the many semantic and technical problems of two fields of science that for the first time find themselves dependent upon each other to help children. Some of these difficulties are outlined here and identify specific areas of need in the medical-educational-mental health-community interface that is developing throughout the country.

THE LEARNING DISABILITIES PHENOMENON

Early in the 1960s psychologists and school personnel began to realize that many children, though not organically retarded, displayed poor achievement and learning skills. These children were a paradox to educators. They were children who appeared intellectually and physically normal but who exhibited specific learning deficits. Medically, such children often displayed subtle signs of neurological deficits that did not affect the entire system, as in mental retardation, but did affect specific areas of language or perceptual capabilities. In most cases, these children evidenced some sort of significant neurological dysfunction that disrupted certain capacities or skills while not causing general incompetence. These children were called children with minimal brain dysfunction. This label indicated a specific neurological difficulty that usually resulted in specific learning problems. Many other terms such as perceptually handicapped, neurologically impaired, and developmental disability were also used, but in each case, medical verification of some sort of neurological dysfunction was required to determine the cause of the learning difficulty; so far, so good. However, once there was public awareness of this subtle and often elusive difficulty, thousands of children who were having learning problems were suspected of having some sort of neurological dysfunction. Once Pandora's box was opened, it was not to be closed, and almost overnight educators and psychologists alike began to classify children with specific learning problems as children who exhibited the minimal brain dysfunction syndrome. It was but a short step to assume that almost any child who did not learn well but who seemed generally normal might have the syndrome. Minimal brain injury quickly became a "learning disability," and the great race was on to develop a whole new educational industry that diagnosed, treated, and resolved learning disabilities. The medical practitioner withdrew in awe and returned to his office, while the educator and psychologist ran about speaking of neurological syndromes that no one in medical school knew existed.

The learning disabilities phenomenon, which occurred for a period roughly covering 1968 to 1978, was a time when specific learning difficulties were suspected of having some sort of subtle neurological basis. While in most cases few if any clear-cut signs of such neurological basis could be found, the whole area of learning disabilities flourished. At present, the phenomenon is somewhat abating due to several of the following factors:

1. Identification of actual neurological deficits of a stuble nature, even when present, is not receptive to general medical procedures and remains essentially an educational issue. If a child has some sort of minimal neurological dysfunction that is not operative or receptive to medication, then the problem is one of how to teach him and not a medical issue at all.
2. Studies of the effectiveness of stimulants in cases of suspected hyperactivity, while demonstrating some relief from incessant behavior, have not demonstrated the solution to the problem. Actual cases of hyperactivity that can be identified as based in actual central nervous system dysfunction are rare. The majority of cases appear related to environmental, social, and personality difficulties. In the majority of cases, the basis of hyperactivity appears to be that of poor parental and behavioral management (Fadely and Hosler, 1979).
3. Schools have developed a range of special programs, curriculum materials, and teaching strategies that do appear to be effective in assisting children with various learning disabilities within the regular school program without extensive special education.
4. Parents and schools have become familiar with the concept of learning disabilities; subsequently, the phenomenon has lost much of its intrigue and mystique. After all is said and done, everyone realizes that these children are children like all others, and the only way to assist them is through the

everyday hard work of parenting and teaching. That is true of every child, learning disabled or not.

5. Finally, but most significantly, it has now been realized that while there are cases of children with real neurological difficulties, most children who appear to be learning disabled are simply children who display differences in developmental competencies or temporary delays in specific developmental abilities.

Generally, then, in the late 1970s, we are seeing that those with learning disabilities include a number of children who deviate from the normal developmental rates in specific areas that are critical to learning in school and adjusting in the community. The learning disabilities movement has been valuable in that it has forced schools and parents to look at the nature of child development in more specific ways and, therefore, adjust school curriculum to the needs of the individual child rather than attempting to teach all children in the same way. Much understanding of development has occurred during this period, and education is much more effective in helping children learn than it once was. However, it will remain for the schools and supporting agencies to provide a good estimate of the nature of a particular child's needs so as to provide an effective program for him.

The future interface between medicine-education-mental health-community will be one in which developmental competencies, physical health, and general family integrity can be assessed and supported.

THE SLOW LEARNER

Many children display difficulties in learning across all curriculum areas. They are not to be considered retarded but, in fact, are so slow in the learning environment that they are unable to compete with or keep abreast of the other children. They slowly fall further behind each year until their difficulties are so great that they give up. They drop out of school, become behavior problems, and show many signs of social and emotional difficulties. To be sure, this group, like those with learning disabilities, displays many signs of specific developmental difficulties. Unlike the learning disabled child, however, these children evidence a pervasive delay in learning and development as opposed to specific areas of deficit. The learning disabilities child usually displays a general level of intellectual functioning within the 90 to 110 IQ range or above with a notable difference between achievement and intelligence. Normal intelligence is considered to be an IQ of 90-110 without the notable difference between verbal and nonverbal scores. Retardation, in most states, is accepted as a general level of intellectual functioning below a 70 IQ level, up to 79 in some states. The slow learner is usually considered that child who shows a general level of functioning within the 80 to 90 IQ range.

The slow learner, then, is a child with a mental age within one to two years below normal. This implies that the child is developing slowly and that he is usually more than a year behind his classmates of the same age relative to general developmental expectations. The reasons for this delay are many, but the important aspect to realize is that there is a general and pervasive delay affecting language and perceptual motor functions. Those who generally compose this group are as follows:

1. Children who come from deprived home environments in which there has been poor parental care, nutritional care, and socialization.
2. Children who display emotional problems and who may have suffered traumatic early childhood problems such as child neglect or abuse, physical disabilities, or premature birth.
3. Children who come from large families in which parenting and individual child care were inadequate due to poor parenting or special circumstances.
4. Children from rural areas where school and community services were inferior or where the family moved often, preventing adequate consistency in early school experience.
5. Children from migrant families who failed to enroll the children in school and did not attend to their children's educational needs.

6. Children with poor genetic or prenatal care, which resulted in generalized poor development within the central nervous system. This can occur, aside from specific genetic defects, from maternal ingestion of drugs during pregnancy, maternal disease transmissions, or other insults to the developing fetus.

The slow learner, twenty years ago, would have simply been considered a "dull" child and little would have been expected of him. He would have been in the back of the room, encouraged not to be too noisy, and he would have remained there grade after grade until he dropped out of school. There were, however, many children who were slow learners in school, who grew up, did graduate from high school, and eventually became productive and responsible members of the community. Perhaps even more startling, many of them did better economically than their teachers.

Today, thanks to increased knowledge and understanding of development, many of the slow-learning children do not sit in the back of the classroom, nor are they sent off to special education diagnosed as mentally retarded. True, many slow learners still drop out of school, many become delinquents, others end up on welfare roles, and still others somehow seem to disappear somewhere into the great stream of humanity, fighting for survival. A larger and larger portion of them, in enlightened schools, are given special methods of learning and resource assistance from traveling teachers. The school curriculum has also changed in ways that assist them, because a critical question was asked of the slow learners. Given an earlier start such as in Head Start Programs, given additional time and special assistance, could such children eventually continue to develop to the point that their delay would no longer be significant? In essence, could these children make up their deficit with assistance? The answer has been a cautious, positive response. The response is cautious because there are so many factors that contribute to the slow development. There are many conditions that inhibit or stimulate possible increase in their developmental rate. One thing is certain; slow learners cannot be ignored, for the cost of not helping them causes society a lifetime of welfare, legal, and occupational payments. They are there and they need everyone's help.

BEHAVIORAL DISORDERS

In recent years an increasing problem in school programs has been children who display a number of behavioral disorders. These range from outright delinquency to minor infractions of school rules. There are children who display great difficulties in following directions, in completing their work, in accepting responsibility, and generally in adhering to expectations of school personnel. While all of these difficulties have a myriad of basic causal factors, there is a general trend that runs through them all — a lack of personal responsibility and personal organization of behavior toward expected learning and behavioral goals. These children are often labeled emotionally disturbed, minimally brain injured, culturally deprived, and any other label that appears to fit at the moment. Some of them may have these difficulties, but in the main none can truly be called anything but — as school teachers did in the "good ole days" — unruly and hard to manage. In our work, for every child we find who has an actual learning disability, who is truly delinquent because of cultural deprivation, or who displays actual personality disorders, we find three who are simply children who exhibit what we call "character or behavioral disorders." They range from the ages of six to sixteen, and for the most part they come from the middle to upper class socially and economically. They exhibit the following characteristics as a group. Some children exhibit all of these difficulties and others only some, but all are severe enough to warrant special attention. They will be seen in medical clinics as well as the mental health clinics, and it is important to identify their behavioral syndrome as distinct from children who exhibit actual cultural deprivation, learning disabilities, or personality problems.

These characteristics include the following:

1. There is normal psychological development.
2. There is normal intellectual functioning.
3. There is distractability and poor attention to task.
4. There is a tendency to avoid school tasks or complete

assignments unless under the direct supervision of an adult.

5. There is usually a tendency to be highly competitive and aggressive.
6. There is a tendency to resist parental and adult authority and to argue or defy adult supervision.
7. There is a high interest in television and high-activity stimulation.
8. There is a tendency to get into arguments and confrontations with peers.
9. The parents are usually conscientious and democratic in their parenting style.
10. The parents tend to avoid physical punishment and often relate to their children in adult ways such as kidding, confronting verbally, using reason, and often give in to their demands for attention or materialistic needs.
11. The family is often a high-activity family with all members heavily involved in athletic, social, and community activities.
12. The mother is often the primary caretaker with the father playing a somewhat passive role. In many cases the family is a single-parent home.
13. The family often does not have a serious religious affiliation or does not attend church at all.
14. The parents display many unmet emotional needs themselves, and tend to fight often or are walled off from each other with a tendency to intellectualize everything rather than express wholesome emotion.

These families are "good families" because they are economically seen as concerned parents and appear to be giving their children the expected home environment that is supposed to be desirable. It does not work. The child in such an environment finds it difficult to accept personal responsibility and tends to be highly competitive as a compensation for feelings of negativism, rejection, and lack of security.

THE EMOTIONALLY DISTURBED

It is interesting that in the last few years, aside from obvious cases such as autistic or psychotic children, there has been less emphasis on the emotional disorders of children and more on the social or learning disorders. It is as if for ten years or so there simply have not been many emotionally disturbed children. Children who have been diagnosed as emotionally disturbed have tended to be the more severe cases that have always been there. However, children with neurotic personalities, those with severe withdrawal and poor adjustment symptoms, and those who tend to be unsocialized and acting out seemed to somehow decrease in frequency. At least this is the case in the schools and to a large degree in the community. Have there actually been less disturbed children who needed special help along with the parents? No, it is simply that for a time we have called them something else, along with the notion that, during the so-called social revolution of the late 1960s and early 1970s, it was somehow fashionable to be strange. It is not that simple, of course, and the following factors appear to have played a strong role in the lack of emphasis on children with personality disorders in the last ten years:

1. During the last decade many children who displayed severe emotional disorders were simply classified as learning disabled from a pseudo-psychoneurological viewpoint. It has not worked, and school personnel are once again beginning to look at personality instead of perceptual and motor problems.

2. During the past decade a much broader range of behavioral deviance has been accepted in every child during the social change that has occurred. For example, it became popular for young people to wear long hair, leather hats, and generally to strive to look like bums. In that atmosphere it became difficult to determine who was well and who was sick. Behavioral standards, dress style, and general values are once again returning to the norm, and those children who are truly unusual are beginning to stand out.

3. Mental health professionals have, due to their own reaction to the social revolution, changed to some degree their analysis of what should be considered abnormal. The authors have been amused during the last ten years to see

many psychologists and psychiatrists join the youth revolution, donning bell-bottom trousers and jean jackets, and sprouting long grey hair down to their shoulders. To some degree it has proven what many have always believed, that people in the mental health field are sometimes not unlike their patients.

4. Concepts in treatment of emotional disorders have changed, and traditional institutionalization, medication, and isolation have become somewhat less needed with the success of many newer sorts of therapy administered within community mental-health clinics.

5. It would appear that many more parents seek professional help early from private practitioners. The patient load for mental health problems in psychologists' and psychiatrists' private offices, and in mental health clinics, has greatly expanded in recent years.

6. School curriculum has changed, and these changes make possible the accommodation of children with a wider range of socioemotional difficulties than schools once served.

There are many children in today's schools who display various forms of emotional difficulties. These are children who possess severe problems with self-concept, who are unable to get along with their peers, and who are severely withdrawn and unresponsive. These are children who do not talk, who refuse to participate; yet, in many cases it is interesting to note that they continue to go to school without any special assistance. One would ask, how is it possible? One ten-year-old girl who attended a rural school did not talk, had not talked since she started school, was severely withdrawn, and was then in the sixth grade. The teacher had called us to school to observe her. It was obvious that the child had a severe problem, but the parents would not consent to any special education or to testing in the school. When the child was younger, the mother had consented to take her to a local medical center, where she was found to be severely disturbed. The parents refused to enter into treatment and since that time had simply sent her to school.

Our case records and our work with schools are filled with many instances in which parents refuse to allow any sort of special treatment for a child who is obviously severely disturbed. Even if a child's parents are willing to submit the child to evaluation at school, in cases of emotional disorders we usually recommend that the school obtain complete medical evaluation from the family physician. If a child has severe emotional difficulties it is important that a full-range evaluation be completed and not just a psychological one. Often the parents will consent to a medical examination when they will not consent to any other sort of evaluation. Thus, both because of the trust the family usually has in their family physician and because of the need for a complete medical examination in any case, it is best if the assessment begins there.

One of the greatest problems in helping children with special problems is assuring that they obtain the proper assistance throughout their life space. It is one thing to determine that a child has a learning disability, but it is another thing to translate that information into communications that assure the follow-through needed to assist the child. A common problem in helping hyperactive children, dyslexic children, and slow learners has been a lack of effective communication between agencies that are involved with the child.

SCHOOL CURRICULUM

Schools have changed and are continuing to change dramatically from the programs that parents attended. Parents are often uncertain as to the meaning of various school programs such as continuous education, individually guided education, ungraded schools, and open schools. Often this lack of understanding is devastating in that many parents rebel against changes that could help their children because the new innovations are so poorly communicated to nonschool personnel.

All children are different. That is a simple statement that has finally revolutionized education. Twenty years ago all children were given much the same curriculum and taught by the same techniques. Regardless of a child's readiness to learn, he had to find some way to cope with what was given him or fail. Children were often grouped into slow, average, or advanced, but this was usually the only differentiation made.

In the individualized process a child with developmental difficulties can be taught in ways that assist his learning process. The more advanced child can be given more complex and supplementary materials, while the teacher gives the less capable child more attention in specific areas of difficulty. Further, many special materials are available in the individualization process that not only assist the child in learning but also may stimulate developmental abilities that are delayed.

Individualization is not complete. Children still work in groups and attend special sessions with the teacher in areas such as science and social studies, where reading skills for all children need not be the same. However, in the development of specific learning skills and later in many supplementary areas, each child works independently with the assistance of the teacher, an older child, or a teacher's aide. The individualization process often allows the child to participate in planning his work schedule, his assignments, and rules for learning. The child accepts responsibility and may write a "contract" for the areas of work he plans to complete. In this way the child is more involved in planning, evaluating, and accounting for his own behavior than in the traditional structure.

In many individualized programs the teacher has to write educational and learning objectives for each child. This becomes a very specific process in which the teacher has to understand each child's needs and structure definite learning goals that are appropriate to those needs. In special education such plans are often called Individual Educational Programs or Plans. It is required by law that these be written. This leads us to the special services and programs that are available to children in today's schools. This brief encounter with the regular classroom illustrates, though, that every child, handicapped or not, in the emerging schools of tomorrow is more and more treated as an individual. As might be suspected, many children who would have had difficulties in the competitive world of yesterday's schools now are often assisted within the regular course of study. There are, however, those children who need even much more than this sort of assistance, and they are children whom the medical practitioner and mental health professional will find requesting their services.

The development of greater understanding of how children

learn and their individual differences has forced education to differentiate curriculum styles far beyond the old concept of slow, average, and advanced. There is not wide agreement, even in education, as to the best general strategies for organizing curriculum. At one end of the continuum is a group that believes that education should focus primarily on basic skills such as reading, writing, and math, while the opposing group feels that it is more important to teach children how to reason, to problem solve, and to deal with their society. Of course, neither concept alone is correct, for schools must do both. The establishment of certain goals for education has always been a controversial and changing problem. There are many schools in the country that still cling primarily to the teaching of the basic concepts. There are newer schools that have thrown out the books altogether and operate on a totally child-centered program. Again, neither approach works for all children, and certainly the nature of the local community determines, to a significant degree, what emphasis shall be given in the schools. A school may run a curriculum counter to the general wishes of the community for a period of time, but eventually the cultural and socioeconomic nature of the community will force the curriculum in the local school toward the community's values and desires. This struggle, schools experimenting with newer concepts of curriculum and parents demanding specifics in the curriculum, is an ongoing and dynamic process that allows both for experimentation and stability over time.

One of the more stable innovations that is being incorporated into more and more schools is a compromise between the more open and traditional schools. The process can be applied in either form of school curriculum and is presently well entrenched in school philosophy should the school count itself "open" or "traditional." The process of individualizing curriculum was originally part of the trend toward open schools where walls, grade levels, and traditional learning classifications were eliminated. Individualization involves developing teaching strategies in which each child is given specific methods of learning fitted to his own needs. This is a very difficult way to teach and demands far more from the teacher than the traditional approaches.

LEGISLATION IN SPECIAL EDUCATION

Both at the federal and state levels, important laws have been passed in recent years that have profoundly affected children with special needs. The laws pertaining to the handicapped designate special services and opportunities that must be available for children within school programs. The exact laws can be obtained by writing to the state educational agencies in all states. It would be good for the medical and mental health clinics to have these on file for reference.

In recent years schools have been required to develop services and programs to assure that handicapped children receive equal opportunity within educational programs. This sort of legislation was particularly important for the severely retarded in that schools have not traditionally considered such children their responsibility. The legislation demanded that schools program these children. The physically handicapped, the deaf, the blind, and other handicapped children have received much more assistance because of such legislation.

The legislation has gone even further, stating that all children with special learning, behavioral, developmental, social, and other handicapping conditions should also receive special assistance. It was further recommended that each child receive such special assistance within the "least restrictive environment." This meant that children with special problems should not be placed in segregated programs but rather kept as close to the mainstream of education as possible. This concept is the now famous, in education, "mainstreaming approach" to serving the handicapped. The belief is that all children will most appropriately learn and develop within the mainstream of society and not in special classrooms isolated from the normal children. To this end many deaf, blind, physically handicapped, and even retarded children now spend much of their time in the regular classrooms and not solely in special programs.

Further, guidelines have been developed nationwide as to how children may qualify for special services, how the schools shall go about evaluating and placing children in programs, and how they shall determine if adequate progress is being made. In essence, the schools have been placed under much direction and stress to provide for special children.

Parent's rights, in the case of the handicapped, have not been neglected either. Parents must agree to any evaluation made of their children, they must be given a case review by school personnel involved who present alternate plans of serving their child, and the parents have to approve the program before it can be initiated. There are special hearing procedures should parents disagree with the school program and the parents may request discontinuation of their child's participation in special education if they so decide.

Appropriate classifications of the nature of special problems that qualify for special services are outlined within each state's own special education legislation. The names of specific services may vary from state to state, but the services available to children other than special state schools and institutions, which are fairly traditional, are as follows:

A. Special segregated classes for
   1. Preschool and elementary through high school students.
   2. Classifications including such areas as mentally retarded, emotionally disturbed, hearing impaired, deaf, visually handicapped, blind, learning disabilities, speech and hearing difficulties, physically handicapped, and home-bound children.
B. Part-time special classes integrated with regular class attendance.
C. Resource teachers, crisis teachers, and itinerant teachers, all of whom provide special part-time assistance for children and teachers in the regular classroom.
D. Special services such as speech and hearing consultants, psychometrics, social services, health care, and economic assistance.
E. State institutions and community centers for day care and twenty-four hour care.

The time is past when most educational, health care, and helping professionals can all do their work with a family regardless of what other professionals are doing. The science of child development and learning, the medical aspects of behavior and development, and the dynamic interactions between child and family, child and school, and child and community require a new form of service to children and their families.

Reference

1. Fadely, Jack L. and Hosler, Virginia N.: *Understanding the Alpha Child at Home and School.* Springfield, Thomas, 1979.

Chapter 4

THE PRESCHOOL CHILD

O UR BASIC CONCERN in this book is with the child from four to twelve years old. Much of the material will be applicable to younger and older children as will be seen by the tests. However, the preschool years are important years, and while there is a great deal of material available on young children prior to the age of four, this is an area that is always difficult for most professionals, since there are so many possible changes over relatively short periods in specific areas of development. Further, it is difficult to evaluate such areas as intelligence, perceptual motor development, and language. Though it is not the intent to focus on this difficult stage of development, some guidelines are given in this chapter that can be added to the many materials and guides most medical and mental health practitioners already have concerning early childhood. Additional discussions will be given over to consideration of four- and five-year-old children in the section covering specific tests and materials. This chapter, while including some discussion of four and five year olds, is primarily intended to provide some general suggestions for the preschool years from eighteen months through kindergarten.

The Denver Developmental Scale is used by many medical and mental health practitioners, and while it provides a quick estimate of many factors, it is so general that often many questions remain. The authors hope that the following materials will add to the Denver and other instruments currently in use.

One of the basic quick-scoring instruments in the areas of language and verbal intelligence, which will be used for children in elementary school, is the Peabody Picture Vocabulary Test. The PPVT is an auditory-visual association intelligence test and correlates somewhat well with full-scale intelligence tests such as the WISC, except that it may tend to score slightly higher (usually no more than 5-10 points higher). Before discussion of the

44

Peabody Picture Vocabulary Test, some general statements should be made about the testing process.

One of the major difficulties in formal evaluation of children is establishing rapport with the child. Particularly in the case of younger children, the examiner needs to spend some time with the mother and the child together to form an initial environment of safety for the child. It is sometimes possible and even desirable to have the parent sit in on the examination. Many professionals who do various types of testing with children often use tests that require, due to the standardization of the test instruments, that the child and examiner be in an isolated and quiet room without distractions. A parent in the room can constitute a major distraction, but, in our practice, we have found that having the mother present is a valuable asset. In the interaction between child and mother and the child's ability to work with the parent, important insights into the child's personality and ability are revealed. Thus, we recommend having the mother sit in the room, though in a position usually to the rear of the child.

Younger children, as opposed to children six years or older, are often much more cautious about strangers, and the younger the child the more this is the case. The examiner should spend a few moments talking to the child and mother and provide toys or other play items. We often begin by asking the child to color a picture, build a tower of blocks, or draw a picture as we spend a few moments talking to the mother. Then, as the atmosphere appears secure, we ask the child to point to some pictures for us (PPVT). The PPVT is a great icebreaking instrument in that the child does not have to perform, and responses can be limited to pointing only.

In many cases, if it is possible in the examining room, a tape recorder assists the examiner in remembering important items until he or she is more familiar with the test instruments and the examination process. Materials that are to be used to test the child should be well laid out, and the general process of evaluation should be organized prior to beginning the examination.

The examiner, particularly with young children, should have several alternate strategies to be used in case one particular test is not well received by the child. Young children also have the distracting habit of turning away during the testing process to go play with a toy or in some manner move off task. The examiner must stay very flexible and if the child appears distracted, move with him, play on the floor for a few moments, talk to him, suggest another activity such as coloring a picture, and slowly move back to the task. Preschool teachers call this process "redirecting the child's attention," and it is important if one is to work with preschool children. Often a direct confrontation such as "stop that" or "do this" will be followed by complete withdrawal of the child or outright refusal to cooperate. It is difficult to complete the evaluation with a young child, and sometimes the parent's report of a child's ability or skill has to be used in some items instead of a direct observation. Remember, the tests are not some sort of sacred ritual; it is information we are after, and the examiner has to work within a loose framework of structure. Sometimes a session has to be discontinued with a promise from the child that he will come back next week to play again. Everyone hates bribes, but with children some sort of treat at the end of the session is highly effective. Not only does it serve to make the child feel secure due to the high oral needs of young children, it is, as the behavioral psychologists like to say, a reinforcement that will tend to cause the behavior to reoccur. We have had many children who work very hard in our office when they are untestable by others. This is because, when needed, there are plenty of oral reinforcers available.

The Peabody Picture Vocabulary Test is a series of pictures in a handbook, which the child looks at as the examiner has him point to particular pictures. There are four pictures on each page, and the child is given one oral stimulus such as "point to the dog, point to the person picking," etc. The child points to the appropriate picture and the examiner moves on to the next page. The Peabody can be administered in five to ten minutes with almost any child between the ages of two and one half and eighteen. For this reason it will be used not only with preschool but with all children. The PPVT uses a basal-age and ceiling-age concept and yields a single IQ score.

Another test that is more complex but, like the PPVT, has a good range of usage is the Zimmerman Preschool Language Scale. This test requires about fifteen to twenty minutes to give but has the advantage of yielding a specific language score rather than an IQ score and, therefore, is more easily related to parents. It works well within the medical environment because it is attuned to developmental ages. It is possible with the Zimmerman to isolate specific areas of difficulty, and it provides for the examiner and the parent some specific factors that are included in language development. It is for children between eighteen months and seven years old. It also includes an articulation test, which is useful when referring a child for a speech and hearing evaluation and for giving the parents specific areas of difficulty.

The Peabody Picture Vocabulary Test and the Zimmerman are two standardized instruments that provide a wide range of information and are excellent supplements to the materials normally used with early childhood assessment procedures. There are many developmental checklists that can be used either through observation or with parental interviews. Often these checklists focus on physiological development and, particularly for young children, insufficient factors are observed. On the following pages we have summarized many recommended developmental lists into one for each age of two, two and one half, three, four, and five years. These are to be used as both an observational and a parent interview form. This list can be duplicated and sent home with the parent to complete over a two-week period. The mental health professional will, during the course of administering the Zimmerman and the PPVT, evaluate many of the factors on the developmental list. This will provide a cross-check and assist in verifying what the parent is reporting.

It should be added that many parents have a tendency to overstate what they believe their child can accomplish. Thus, it might be felt that having a parent complete the checklist at home would tend to provide less than objective material. If parents do overstate their child's abilities and skills, they first of all will be aware of this even though they feel they are being objective. The point of having them complete the checklist at home is to get them to look specifically at their child's behavior. The possibility that they may overstate is not so important that the checklist should not be used. Further, our experience suggests that the parents are more likely to be uncertain of a child's ability than they are to overstate it. When the checklist is reviewed with the parents following their evaluation, their questions and the interaction that the checklist allows between themselves and the examiner open up many worthwhile discussions. Again, the point of the examination is not only to discover special needs of a child but to assist the parents in understanding their child better. The checklist provides a form of parent education. Specific areas of learning or developmental needs can be brought to the attention of the child's preschool teacher or day care worker who, during the course of working with a child, can focus on these specific concerns.

PHYSIOLOGICAL SYSTEM SURVEY

2 Years

Physical Development

____ 1. Sturdy on feet and bends at the waist to pick up an object
____ 2. Goes up and down stairs but without alternating feet
____ 3. Can kick a ball
____ 4. Can take simple things apart and put them back together
____ 5. Can rotate forearm and therefore turn door knob
____ 6. Can draw a crude circle by imitation
____ 7. Can build a tower of 6-7 blocks with difficulty
____ 8. Can put on shoes, socks, and pants
____ 9. Usually dry at night
____ 10. Runs but is unable to make sudden stops or turn easily
____ 11. Alternates between standing and sitting easily
____ 12. Tends to be motorically active and exploratory

Social Development

____ 13. Pinches, bites, kicks, and pushes
____ 14. Does not share; is very possessive
____ 15. Solitary rather than cooperative play — begins parallel play
____ 16. Shy with strangers

_____ 17. Alternates between dependent and independent behavior
_____ 18. Enjoys imitation
_____ 19. More responsive to distraction and humor than discipline

---

Personality and Cognitive Development

_____ 20. Negative and assertive
_____ 21. Cannot make choices
_____ 22. Fear of wetting the bed and animals; helpless in the face of threat
_____ 23. Fussy eater
_____ 24. Self-centered and ritualistic
_____ 25. Shows empathy, shame, and can evidence guilt
_____ 26. Can show great affection
_____ 27. Intrigued with water
_____ 28. Ideas and perceptual awareness more developed than physical abilities
_____ 29. Some willingness to do for others
_____ 30. Can wait or suffer temporary frustration

Language Development

_____ 31. Vocabulary of 50-250 words
_____ 32. Can point to ten pictures when told to find them in a book
_____ 33. Obeys one or two prepositions; put on, under, in
_____ 34. Identifies five body parts
_____ 35. Uses some verbs, adjectives, and nouns
_____ 36. Is possessive; uses word *mine* frequently
_____ 37. Articulation 60 to 75 percent intelligible
_____ 38. Calls self by first name
_____ 39. Asks for food, drink, and toilet
_____ 40. Can repeat a three-word sentence
_____ 41. Recognizes body parts on a doll
_____ 42. Follows simple directions
_____ 43. Identifies several pictures from question: "What is this?"

_____ 44. Names objects in environment

---

2 ½ Years

Physical Development

_____ 1. Jumps forward on both feet

_____ 2. Can walk on tiptoes

_____ 3. Can build a tower of 8 blocks and simple structures

_____ 4. Can imitate vertical and horizontal pencil strokes

_____ 5. Stands on one foot for more than 2 seconds

_____ 6. Jumps from a chair

_____ 7. Fair hand and finger coordination — holds pencil correctly

_____ 8. Can move fingers independently

_____ 9. Can make simple drawings

Social Development

_____ 10. Negativism at peak

_____ 11. Much continued ritualism

_____ 12. Often cannot make a choice; stalls

_____ 13. Dramatic and parallel play

Personality and Cognitive Development

_____ 14. Goes to extremes in most things

_____ 15. Frequent use of "I will," or "I won't"

_____ 16. Attempts to do both things rather than making choice

_____ 17. Cannot be forced

_____ 18. Impatient and wants mother to do

_____ 19. Likes routine and security; does not want to do new things

_____ 20. Wants a particular spoon; may cry until needs are met

_____ 21. Distracted by multiplicity

Language Development

_____ 22. Points to 15 pictures

_____ 23. Obeys prepositions
_____ 24. Sounds *t, d, k, g, ng,* in words
_____ 25. Can repeat two digits
_____ 26. Can remember two objects
_____ 27. 400-800 words in vocabulary
_____ 28. Uses nouns, verbs, adjectives, and the pronoun *I*
_____ 29. Uses three words in a sentence
_____ 30. Identifies objects by use
_____ 31. Answers questions about what you do with specific objects
_____ 32. Understands the concept of one
_____ 33. Follows simple commands
_____ 34. Names many objects in the environment
_____ 35. Can repeat simple sentences

General Health

_____ 36. Elimination and retention difficulty
_____ 37. Need for accessory object at night
_____ 38. Some thumb sucking or masturbating
_____ 39. Stuttering may be prevalent in high-language children
_____ 40. Completely disrupts playroom
_____ 41. Sudden aggressive acts
_____ 42. Temper tantrums

2½ Years — Developmental Milestones Related to Learning

_____ 1. General balance improves and able to balance on tiptoes with increased motor control.
_____ 2. Able to organize motor behavior into vertical and horizontal space. Basis for later organization in space and time.
_____ 3. Able to suspend movement, balancing on one side of the body using lateral stress to maintain position.
_____ 4. Basic development of body control in space.
_____ 5. Accumulating information so rapidly that he must make decisions.
_____ 6. Ego strength reaches level of self-assertion and resistance to external force.

_____ 7. Final stage of motoric sophistication begun with finger dexterity.

_____ 8. Structures complete thought abstractly in simple phrases.

_____ 9. Able to exhibit emotion in play.

_____ 10. Able to mimic complex sentence structure in preparation for personal expression.

_____ 11. Increased ability to associate language structure with meaning of objects in at least their behavior and use.

_____ 12. Increases exploratory recognition of physical self and body parts, which tends to strengthen self-awareness and identification.

_____ 13. Initial stages of recognition of others and interaction

_____ 14. Sequential memory function beginning

---

3 Years

Physical Development

_____ 1. Quite nimble on feet; climbs, runs, turns well, and swings arms like an adult

_____ 2. Rides a tricycle

_____ 3. Dresses and undresses if helped with buttons and can brush teeth

_____ 4. Copies circle and imitates cross

_____ 5. Can draw a man on request

_____ 6. Feeds self well

_____ 7. Full set of temporary teeth

_____ 8. Tiptoes three yards

_____ 9. Walks up stairs with alternating feet

_____ 10. Diagram drawing stage; shapes leading to design combining

---

Social Development

_____ 11. Parallel play with some cooperative play

_____ 12. Begins to wait for turn

_____ 13. Likes to run errands

_____ 14. Distinguishes between boys and girls

_____ 15. Interest in body
_____ 16. Loves to be with other children
_____ 17. Does not share willingly
_____ 18. Ritualism decreases
_____ 19. Begins to use words to comply with cultural demands
_____ 20. Can say "yes" and interested in behavior of others
_____ 21. Will give up objects to gain favor
_____ 22. Can do things others like

Language, Personality, and Cognitive Development

_____ 23. Can count to 5 or 10 but does not understand
_____ 24. Knows night from day
_____ 25. Points to 25 pictures and names 20
_____ 26. *y, f, v,* in words
_____ 27. Can repeat three digits and four-word sentences
_____ 28. 800-1200 words in vocabulary
_____ 29. Pronouns, *you* and *me,* as well as plurals and adjectives
_____ 30. Sentences are usually four or more words
_____ 31. Uses plurals
_____ 32. Announces actions, gives full name and sex
_____ 33. Arranges doll furniture in meaningful groups
_____ 34. Responds to commands of walk, run, and jump
_____ 35. Tells simple action in pictures
_____ 36. Deals with ego-oriented sentence in abstract: "What do you do when sleepy?"
_____ 37. Gives irrelevant responses to difficult questions: "What swims?" A house
_____ 38. Enumerates three objects when asked about a picture
_____ 39. Discriminates between big and little
_____ 40. Distinguishes prepositions *on, in, in front of, under*
_____ 41. Distinguishes parts of objects
_____ 42. Compares sizes
_____ 43. Recognizes time by activity; routine oriented
_____ 44. Matches sets in blocks and colors
_____ 45. Groups animals and toys
_____ 46. Begins to show self-control
_____ 47. Tries to please and conform

_____ 48. Temper tantrums at peak
_____ 49. Imaginary worries; fears dark, dogs, and death
_____ 50. Curiosity level rises
_____ 51. Frustrated with obstacles
_____ 52. Restless sleep
_____ 53. Enjoys praise
_____ 54. Playmates are the main source of anger

General Health

_____ 55. Expresses marked fatigue
_____ 56. Thumb sucking
_____ 57. May wander house at night

---

3 Years — Developmental Milestones Related to Learning

_____ 1. General balance and lateral integration quite developed
_____ 2. Self-care skills greatly increased
_____ 3. Can now demonstrate circle, horizontal, and vertical motor movements
_____ 4. Integration of two motoric sides and top-bottom developed
_____ 5. Drawing complex designs; combinations of shapes
_____ 6. Interest in social values and gaining social approval
_____ 7. Development of basic abstraction in language
_____ 8. Aware of simple perceptual relationships and similarities
_____ 9. Sexual identification through body and activity
_____ 10. Awareness of numbers and counting well initiated
_____ 11. Visual sequential memory basis established
_____ 12. Learning social manipulation
_____ 13. Structuring language to discuss and explore new information; entering perceptual conceptual stage
_____ 14. Development of basic concepts of time and space
_____ 15. Development of basic spatial-language concepts

4-5 Years

Physical Development

_____ 1. Beginning to skip and do stunts
_____ 2. Climbs well
_____ 3. Can cut on a line, throw overhanded, and lace shoes
_____ 4. Holds brush like an adult and paints in flourishes with much conversation
_____ 5. Knows some colors
_____ 6. Jumps over rope
_____ 7. Hops on right or left foot
_____ 8. Catches ball in arms
_____ 9. Walks on line
_____ 10. Draws a man with head, trunk, and legs
_____ 11. Copies a cross
_____ 12. More interested in mixing colors and experimenting than in design
_____ 13. Good fine motor control

Social Development

_____ 14. Endless questions of how and why
_____ 15. Great fabrication
_____ 16. Cooperative play with rapid change in friends
_____ 17. Swearing and silly words
_____ 18. Concern for origin of babies and death
_____ 19. Loves an audience and talks to self if none available
_____ 20. Runs topic into ground
_____ 21. Begins to rationalize
_____ 22. Total confidence in his ability to do anything
_____ 23. Imagination varied and vivid

Language, Personality, and Cognitive Development

_____ 24. Uncontrolled aggression
_____ 25. Love of opposite-sex parent
_____ 26. Name-calling added to tantrums
_____ 27. Defies parents but often quotes them as authorities

____ 28. Acts out if he does not get his way
____ 29. Perceives praise but not as sensitive to it as previously
____ 30. Moralistic judgments begin
____ 31. Out of bounds often until he reaches late fourth year
____ 32. Loud silly laughter at one time, anger at another
____ 33. Perceives analogies
____ 34. Boastful, dogmatic, bossy
____ 35. Begins to conceptualize and generalize
____ 36. Difficulty in separation of fantasies and reality
____ 37. Asserts independence
____ 38. Obeys four or five prepositions
____ 39. Knows what familiar animals do
____ 40. *sh, th,* in words
____ 41. Uses past tense and comparatives
____ 42. Complex sentences of more than five words
____ 43. Relates experiences and seeks information
____ 44. Articulation 90 percent intelligible
____ 45. Errors in *l, r, s, z, ch, j, th*
____ 46. Gives multiple responses to questions
____ 47. Can classify and categorize
____ 48. Understands simple relationships; boy is to brother, as girl is to sister
____ 49. Understands simple cause and effect
____ 50. Can explain words like *shoe, knife, bicycle, hat*
____ 51. Repeats sentences
____ 52. Knows opposites
____ 53. Counts to ten
____ 54. Understands senses
____ 55. Concept of 3 developed
____ 56. Touches thumbs together on demand
____ 57. Comprehends remote events

General Health

____ 58. Catches many colds
____ 59. Has stomachaches in social situations
____ 60. Needs to urinate at inconvenient times
____ 61. May begin losing front teeth

_____ 62. Has nightmares and fears

_____ 63. May spit, bite, and kick

4-5 Years — Developmental Milestones Related to Learning

_____ 1. General coordination integrated into language; has many automatic behavioral motor responses that do not need to be concentrated on

_____ 2. Able to balance and exhibit control in off-ground activities

_____ 3. Orients to space and time; "I jumped yesterday"

_____ 4. Rapid integration of many motor and language functions

_____ 5. Becomes more ego-centered and conscious of self in relation to others

_____ 6. Strong beginning on cultural values

_____ 7. Actively using language to acquire new information

_____ 8. Begins to see perceptual and abstract relationships

---

5 Years

Physical Development

_____ 1. Has good general posture

_____ 2. Can skip

_____ 3. Can balance on either foot

_____ 4. Runs, jumps, and can hop on one foot

_____ 5. Can climb two body lengths

_____ 6. Can do three jumping jacks

_____ 7. Can throw and catch a ball

_____ 8. Can do five sit-ups

_____ 9. Can forward jump on one foot

_____ 10. Can run 50 yards in 20 seconds

Sensory Motor Development

_____ 11. Grasps pencil appropriately

_____ 12. Can copy a circle

_____ 13. Can copy a square

_____ 14. Can copy a triangle
_____ 15. Can draw a person
_____ 16. Displays use of preferred hand
_____ 17. Can cut, color, and paste within boundaries
_____ 18. Can fold paper diagonally
_____ 19. Can draw a line between two lines ½ inch apart transversing a page
_____ 20. Can copy numbers and letters

Auditory Perceptual Development

_____ 21. Can repeat a series of five digits
_____ 22. Discriminates prefix and suffix sounds
_____ 23. Understands auditory directions
_____ 24. Comprehends auditory information
_____ 25. Recognizes similarities and differences
_____ 26. Can repeat sentences
_____ 27. Can repeat rhythm sequence
_____ 28. Understands words spoken in a whisper
_____ 29. Can imitate a variety of sounds
_____ 30. Responds verbally in conversation

Language Conceptual Abilities

_____ 31. Can point to all body parts
_____ 32. Can describe behavior in abstract terms
_____ 33. Recognizes senses
_____ 34. Discriminates between right and left
_____ 35. Demonstrates positive self-concept
_____ 36. Uses personal pronouns: *I, me, you, we*
_____ 37. Sees self as important and is independent
_____ 38. Demonstrates use of objects through movement
_____ 39. Compares self to siblings or peers
_____ 40. Demonstrates general knowledge

Psychosocial Development

_____ 41. Even tempered with stable responses

_____ 42. Seldom cries inappropriately
_____ 43. Not self-conscious with adults
_____ 44. Does not depend on adult direction
_____ 45. Initiates verbal interaction with others
_____ 46. Shares toys and possessions
_____ 47. Can adapt behavior to situation
_____ 48. Willing to join groups
_____ 49. Modifies behavior with experience
_____ 50. Expresses positive and negative feelings
_____ 51. Original and creative in activity
_____ 52. Energetic in learning
_____ 53. Verbalizes well in peer interactions
_____ 54. Organizes activities and follows through
_____ 55. Can postpone gratification
_____ 56. Recovers easily from anger and frustration
_____ 57. Is not easily led into mischief
_____ 58. Resourceful
_____ 59. Empathetic
_____ 60. Has good self-identity

Visual Perceptual Development

_____ 61. Can discriminate between various letters
_____ 62. Knows colors and can match or group colors
_____ 63. Can group objects by size, shape, and color
_____ 64. Can retain and repeat sequential groupings
_____ 65. Adequate visual tracking skills
_____ 66. Adequate visual convergence
_____ 67. Adequate visual focus and scanning
_____ 68. Adequate visual fixation
_____ 69. Can recognize visual similarities
_____ 70. Can recognize parts and wholes of forms and objects

Verbal Expressive Ability

_____ 71. Can describe and tell about familiar objects
_____ 72. Can relate familiar story
_____ 73. Can give accurate description of personal experience

____ 74. Can sing a simple song

____ 75. Asks questions and listens to answers

____ 76. Can give directions to others

____ 77. Can make up pretend stories

____ 78. Can imitate affectual tone in stories or play

____ 79. Can describe personal behavior during performance

____ 80. Can vary intensity and tone of voice appropriately

Conceptual Language Ability

____ 81. Can explain familiar words

____ 82. Associates like and unlike words

____ 83. Can group objects by length, size, shape, and use

____ 84. Can discriminate weights

____ 85. Identifies self by sex, age, and name

____ 86. Recognizes times of day

____ 87. Can pretend to be an adult, parent, or other role model

____ 88. Understands longest, biggest, most, and same

____ 89. Recognizes words about position in space

____ 90. Can place objects in groups of one to ten

General Information

____ 91. Accepts responsibility for self

____ 92. Able to feed self

____ 93. Able to dress self

____ 94. Can tie shoes

____ 95. Washes hands before meals

____ 96. Can provide full name, address, and phone number

____ 97. Energy level sufficient and eats well

____ 98. Health is generally good

____ 99. Graceful in physical activities

____ 100. General behavior appropriate for sex

Test References

1. *Zimmerman Preschool Language Scale*
   Charles Merrill Publishing Company
   1300 Alum Creek Dr.
   Columbus, Ohio 43216

2. *Peabody Picture Vocabulary Test*
   American Guidance Service
   Publishers Building
   Circle Pines, Minnesota 55014
3. *Denver Developmental Screening Test*
   University of Colorado Medical Center
   Denver, Colorado

Chapter 5

PERCEPTUAL MOTOR DEVELOPMENT

THE ASSESSMENT of the perceptual motor function, developmentally, is quite different from assessment of physical
growth, general physical health, or motor coordination. When
looking at a child's general physical development we are not
usually concerned with what may be called "perceptual motor
development" from the standpoint of learning and general behavior. An assessment of perceptual motor development requires an understanding of the relationship between general
physical development, specific motoric and perceptual skills,
and learning, which will consummate in the capacity to learn
formal skills in school.

There are several important motor skills that are usually related to school achievement and adjustment. In the past, because
school and psychological personnel were unaware of the tre-
mendous variation in the developmental rates of perceptual
motor function among children, difficulties in perceptual motor
skills were too often misdiagnosed as learning disabilities. In
fact, as we mentioned earlier, many such children so diagnosed
were simply displaying normal variations in developmental
rates. Assessment of perceptual motor development is usually
accomplished by having the child perform a number of general
physical activities and pencil-paper tasks. These are presented
here for the mental health professional to use within the office.
It must be understood that all such assessments are tentative and
should be used within the context of a general assessment.
Sometimes there is a relationship between specific learning skills
and perceptual motor difficulties and sometimes there is not. In
short, even though a child may have some delay in the development of perceptual motor skills, this does not always imply that
he will have difficulties in school. For the mental health professional, it is important to obtain a case history and a review of
school performance before ascribing any learning-skill signifi-

cance to a particular level of perceptual motor skill. There *is* a general relationship, though, and this should be viewed as such, rather than thinking the specific perceptual motor difficulties in themselves have great importance. The following factors are usually of significance in looking at perceptual motor function.

GENERAL BODY AWARENESS AND CONCEPT

This implies that the child is aware of his body parts, that he is able to distinguish one side from the other, and usually that he is able to name his body parts and specific directions such as left and right.

NEUROLOGICAL DIFFERENTIATION — LATERALITY

This designates that the child has differentiated the various planes of the body and is able to differentially move or coordinate the various parts in an efficient manner. The young child slowly develops coordinated movement upon a kinesthetic feedback mechanism whereby he is aware and able to move specific body parts either individually or in coordination. For example, the child who has adequate kinesthetic differentiation is able to "sense" body movements through recognition of muscle feedback to the central nervous system. The child who "senses" such movement efficiently has differentiated movement well and is able to balance and use muscle groups well. The child who has poor body awareness and poor differentiation will take longer to be able to recognize specific kinesthetic feedback, which will in turn delay correcting movements, and he will have poor balance and movement. This is not an easy thing to assess simply by watching the child walk, since most children have enough practice in general movements so that walking, running, and even hopping appear fairly normal. Yet, when put in stressful situations that require accurate balance and coordination, they display much difficulty. This is why so many children appear capable but later reveal scientific learning problems that are unexpected. More will be discussed concerning this function further on. Laterality is the name usually applied to this internal awareness and capability in kinesthetic skill.

PERCEPTUAL MOTOR ORGANIZATION — DIRECTIONALITY

Based on internal body awareness, recognition of body sides and planes, i.e. up, down, beside, behind, the child comes to identify spatial planes outside of himself. He names space in relation to his own internal organization. In this way there becomes a left side, an up, down, around, behind, and so forth. Directionality is the name given to this awareness. Neurological differentiation comes first, then an awareness of body parts and positions, next the naming of formalized space known as spatial awareness. Space comes to be identified by the child as he becomes more and more capable of naming and responding to it.

MOTORIC DOMINANCE

Very early — at birth many suggest — but at least by the age of three years the young child has chosen a dominant hand. It is, in behavioral terms, a seemingly uncomplicated thing. Yet, this is one of the most significant milestones of the third and fourth year. Many children will persist into the sixth year still uncertain as to their dominant hand. However, by the age of three years, though there may still be much use of the nondominant hand, the child shows definite preference for one hand or the other. Establishment of hand dominance gives space and directionality a particularly definite point of reference, which cannot be established without motoric dominance. Once dominance is established, the child uses that reference point to determine directions and to initiate practice in many fine and gross motor functions. The right-handed child will find later fine motor and spatial organization easier in that most of his world is organized in this manner. The right hand, developmentally, is programmed to work in a predominantly left-to-right fashion while the left hand is organized in a predominantly right-to-left fashion.

The left-handed child may have difficulty establishing good directionality. He may have no difficulty in general movement patterns, but when he has to orient the making of fine motor movements such as in writing, from left to right, this is when he becomes confused and makes reversals. Most children work this out by the age of seven, though some reversals may persist until eight or nine years. Even many right-handed children will reverse letters and numbers during the fifth year, but usually this is quickly overcome. There are many problems related to dominance in the learning environment. Dominance in motoric function, as might be suspected, relates to the establishment of directionality in that there is a specific reference point in space. The ability to relate space in directions leads to the ability to organize the space into segments and from there to the development of a concept of time. The past usually is related to the left or to the rear of a person while the future is related to the right or front of the individual. This provides a basis for organizing sequential language structure. All this suggests that it is important for the child to establish dominance as early as possible and certainly prior to entering school. Children who establish dominance late often have difficulties not only in fine motor reversals but also in time, sequential learning, and following directions.

GENERAL BALANCE AND COORDINATION

Kinesthetic proficiency, laterality, directionality, and motor dominance all contribute to the child's ability to move through space in coordinated and fluid motions. Not only is this important to general play and exploratory behavior, it is important for social acceptance from peers, in early school-learning activities, and eventually in the various abilities involved in sports and school. While a child may develop an adequate motoric basis for coordination, he still has to practice and involve himself in activities that develop skills in these areas. Through parent observations and evaluation in the clinic, the child's general coordination can usually be assessed without any formal testing. However, balance and coordination will be measured throughout several of the following activities and tests.

VISUAL-MOTOR COORDINATION

The child develops general coordination in large muscle groups, and this competency gives rise to ever more detailed fine muscle movements, which eventuate in the various school-related tasks such as copying, drawing, writing, and even reading. The eyes are dependent upon small muscles and are prone to the same difficulties that are experienced in gross motor difficulties. For example, the child who has established poor directionality often displays difficulty in knowing where to look when he is using the fine muscles, and he also may have trouble coordinating the movements of the eyes with the movements of the body, particularly the hands. The left-handed child and the child with general coordination difficulties often have trouble following a moving target, following the hands with the eye or vice versa, and maintaining constant tracking movements with the eyes while writing or reading. This is not a vision problem, though the child may also have vision difficulties, but a coordination problem. This is one of the common sorts of difficulties children with learning disabilities involving perceptual motor skills seem to exhibit. Development of improved perceptual motor function and practice in visual tasks will usually improve this ability.

Assessment of perceptual motor skills should always be preceded by a quick analysis of general intellectual and language functioning, because retarded children or children very slow in language areas may display both difficulties in understanding the task and actual perceptual motor problems. The learning disabilities child is usually considered a child who, though there is normal or near-normal intellectual ability, is having trouble with specific learning problems. Thus, such a child will demonstrate perceptual motor problems that are inconsistent with general intellectual abilities. The slow child has difficulty understanding and performing the task, while the learning disabilities child understands the task but has difficulties performing it and often becomes very frustrated. The slow child more often than not does not know he is not doing well and, thus, is less likely to become frustrated.

GENERAL ASSESSMENT PROCEDURES

In the preceding chapter, many specific aspects of perceptual motor development were listed for the child under six. For the child over six it is more difficult to define specific functions because after six there is much more integration of specific functions, and the tasks required of the child in school require more complex behaviors. Thus, many of the general assessment procedures, while making apparent many aspects of various specific functions, usually involve clusters of behavior from which inferences concerning abilities have to be made.

Balance and General Kinesthetic Skill

There are several activities that can be accomplished with the child who is between six and twelve years; older children can also be given these activities, which will demonstrate basic balance and kinesthetic skills. The first activity that should be included is having the child stand on one foot. He should be able to do so for several seconds, usually six seconds or more for the younger child, and up to ten seconds for the late-elementary-aged child, without falling or having an undue problem. The child with balance problems will often show some difficulty at once and will resort to some constant twisting and movement to maintain balance. This is not a fine sophisticated test, and one should not be concerned about how to score it. Rather, it is a general test, and if the child is able to maintain balance fairly easily then no problem is assumed to exist at this point. If there is an obvious difficulty, then is is assumed that there may be some problem with balance. There is a second phase of the balancing activity, which is even more important than the first. After the child has attempted to stand on one foot he is then asked to do it again but this time with his eyes closed. Many children and adults can maintain minimal levels of coordination and balance while using their eyes, but when they close their eyes they have great difficulty. This is because if we have poor kinesthetic feedback and corrective response, then we often compensate to a large degree by using visual cues instead of kinesthetic cues. By watching where we are in space, along with attending to kinesthetic cues, we can concentrate on maintaining at least minimal balance. Thus, when the child stands on one foot with his eyes closed he has to rely just on kinesthetic cues. Obviously the child who has difficulty balancing with his eyes open will usually have even more difficulty with them closed.

Dominant Eye — Dominant Hand

This assessment will include having the child stand in front of the examiner and hold both hands out in front of his head with the palms up and facing the examiner. Then he is asked to extend the index fingers and the thumbs of each hand, overlapping them. In doing so he forms a small hole about the size of a quarter. He is instructed to look through the hole with both eyes at the examiner's nose. The exercise gives a good assessment of his dominant eye. The child feels he is actually looking through the hole with both eyes, but he will almost always sight with the dominant eye. This is noted on his chart. Later the examiner will note the dominant hand as the child performs copying tasks.

Directional Ability

Spatial and directional ability will be assessed in several different ways throughout the perceptual-motor examination. At this point, while the child continues to stand in front of the examiner, he is asked to touch his left ear with his right hand. This involves not only his ability to relate verbal names to directions but also to his basic awareness of body concept. Children will often touch their right ear with their left hand if they have directional difficulties. Left-handed children are prone to do this but so are children with directional and spatial organization difficulties. The behavior is observed and noted. Some of the common problems include the one just mentioned, but some children also switch two or three times trying to remember which is left and which is right; others touch the ear on the same side as the hand they use, and still others do not seem to understand the directions. All of these difficulties with a child six years or older should provide some suspicion of possible perceptual motor difficulties.

Body Concept and Directionality

A good exercise, particularly for a child under the age of nine years, is angels in the snow. This involves having him lie on the floor with his hands down to his sides. The directions are given three ways. First the directions are given verbally, then visually, and finally kinesthetically. The exercises are given in three stages with a variety of alterations between stages to assure the examiner that any problems noted are truly problems and not simply some difficulty in initially understanding the directions. The first level, which is the simplest, is having the child raise one

limb and then lower it back to the floor. Some examiners have
the child move the limbs out to the side away from the body, but
we have found that having the child raise the limb is just as
effective and is often easier to accomplish. The child is asked to
raise each limb by giving directions such as, "raise the left arm,"
"lift the right leg," etc. The second level of difficulty involves
moving two limbs on the same side of the body at the same time,
for example, "raise your left arm and left leg." The third level
involves raising contralateral limbs, for example, "raise your left
arm and right leg."

The examiner is, in the verbal form, attempting to see if the
child can move the limbs by translating verbal commands into
body movements. This is an auditory-to-motor function. This
simply means, can the child hear and understand the concrete
meaning of a verbal command. The order in which these are
used does not really matter as long as the examiner notes any
difference in performance when directions are given verbally,
visually, or kinesthetically.

The second phase of evaluation is to ask the child to perform
the same three levels of function except that this time the child
watches as the examiner gives the directions by pointing to the
child's body part, which he is supposed to move. The examiner
first points to one limb at a time such as the left arm, then the
right leg, the right arm, and so forth. The second level, as in the
verbal phase, involves pointing to both the left leg and the left
arm and then the right leg and the right arm. Finally, the examiner points to the left arm and the right leg and then the right
arm and the left leg. In this exercise the examiner is evaluating
the child's ability to transfer visual spatial cues into motoric
responses. This is a visual-to-motor function and is somewhat
easier than the verbal-to-motor function because the child has to
transfer abstract verbal cues into motoric cues.

The final phase involves kinesthetic-to-motor function and is
often the easiest, since the child is more likely to respond to
tactile kinesthetic stimulation as a cue to move a particular part
of the body. In order of difficulty, the processes involved are the
most difficult, verbal to motor; next, visual to motor; and the
easiest, kinesthetic to motor. In the kinesthetic-to-motor phase,

the child is asked to close his eyes so that only kinesthetic cues will be used. The examiner then goes through each of the three levels again, single limb, same-side combination, and cross-body arm and leg. The examiner lightly touches the part or parts to be moved. If there is difficulty in the kinesthetic-to-motor phase it is most likely that the other two phases will also display some problem.

At the end of the chapter is a general checklist for this and other screening activities that are not part of a specific test purchased commercially. Supplementary tests that may be added to the battery by the examiner are also included at the end of this section and of each of the others so that those individuals who wish to extend their skills can do so. As often as possible, though, in each section activities are given that can provide an adequate screening procedure, with commercial tests playing only a partial role in the total process of evaluation. It must be remembered that the screening procedures in this book are intended to provide a range of activities whereby the examiner can make a general assessment. It is not intended that the materials here will be in-depth instruments or procedures. Where specific sorts of neurological, developmental, and learning problems are noted the examiner will request additional outside assistance.

Visual Skills

Visual skills are not to be confused with vision acuity testing. Developmentally, the first visual skill that occurs is scanning. This is exhibited in a child's ability to move his eyes about his environment and locate himself in relationship to the things about him. The second developmental skill to occur is that of visual pursuit. This is a child's ability to look at and focus on an object and then follow its path. This is exhibited when a child follows, with his eye, the flight of a bird or bubbles as they drift about. The third developmental visual skill level is that of linear tracking, and this is the level that is most often assessed. This involves the child's ability to move the eyes in a coordinated manner during both monocular and binocular activities. A simple procedure used by many professionals in schools and clinics is to ask the child to "track" a moving object while the examiner watches the eyes to observe general efficiency of movement. This can be accomplished with a simple penlight, which is moved slowly in arcs on vertical, horizontal, and oblique or diagonal planes in front of the child. Usually the child is sitting for this exercise, and the examiner sits in front of the child. The child is asked not to move his head as he follows the penlight. The penlight is held approximately 10 inches in front of the child and then moved up and down in an arc, making sure that the light is moved in a continuous path from top to bottom. The arc extends above the child's head and back down below his chin level. The vertical plane is usually the easiest for the child to accomplish in that the vertical eye and head movements are first to mature. Next the arc is made on the horizontal plane and is moved back and forth at about the speed one watches a tennis ball during a tennis match or a free-swinging ball on a string. As the child follows the penlight in a horizontal plane, the examiner watches to see if the child loses sight of the light and must search for it, if he continues to move his eyes to the left or the right and does not stop as the light is moved in the other direction, or if the child tends to move only one eye. The oblique movement is the last to mature, and testing of it is done by moving the penlight in both left and right diagonal movement arcs over the left and right shoulders. All four arcs make a pattern as shown on the next page.

Following the linear tracking exercises the child is asked to watch the light and tell the examiner when he sees two lights. The penlight is held directly in front of the child's nose and moved slowly toward the nose from a position approximately 20 inches away. As the light is moved in the examiner watches to see if the child moves both eyes in or if only one eye follows the target as well as noting the recovery rate of the eyes back to a normal position. The penlight should then be moved out again, watching to see if both eyes follow. This is done several times, and the eye that most often makes the inward movement is noted. In many cases the child may do fairly well when the light is moved in, and then one eye or the other will break away prematurely. There are many errors in linear tracking and convergence that may be noted. When attempting convergence the following may be noted:

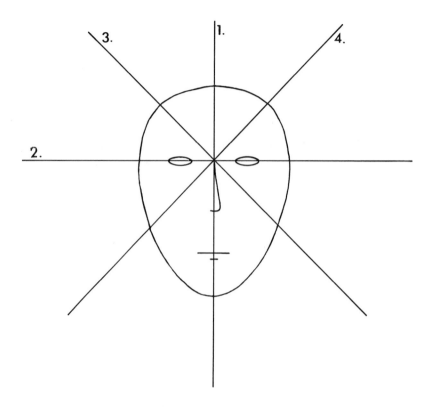

1. Only one eye will come in to the point of convergence while the other wanders.
2. Both eyes will converge, but only one eye will be able to follow the outward movement.
3. Both eyes will start to converge, but one will stop moving toward the point of convergence.
4. As the eyes converge a point will be reached where both eyes appear to tire and they simply move outward, seemingly not under the child's control, to their normal position.
5. The child will not see two penlights as the light is moved in but will report two objects as the penlight is moved out.

When attempting linear tracking exercises the following may be noted:

1. The eyes may move smoothly up to the mid-line and at that point appear to jerk and continue on smoothly.
2. On the left side of the mid-line the left eye may appear to be tracking while the right eye deviates. As you cross the mid-line to the right side the right eye may track while the left eye deviates.
3. The child may have only one eye that will track.

This simple exercise has one major drawback — examiners often place too much emphasis on difficulties seen during such activity. This is an artificial activity and one that requires near-vision function. The younger the child the more likely some difficulties will be seen. Thus, when young children of three to five years are being evaluated, difficulties should be noted but care taken not to overreact to them. Yet, this exercise often does provide valuable indicators of difficulties in the learning environment. Usually, if problems are present it is not a case of some sort of medical problem but rather that the child's eyes have simply not matured enough for near-vision tasks of any duration.

There are several reasons why this area, if difficulties are noted, may not pose any problem for the child. Some children quickly learn, when they have difficulty with tracking and convergence skills, that they can use one eye more efficiently than two in near-vision tasks. Such a child will often lay his head on his arm during reading, drawing, or writing and thereby block out the nondominant eye, thus simply making a mechanical compensation. It is important, then, to watch the child during reading, writing, and other tasks that involve near vision during the remainder of the examination. Visual difficulties may be indicated if the child attempts to block the eye by laying his head on an arm on his desk, by turning the head, or even by holding one hand on the side of the face. These tendencies to compensate *usually* suggest a child who is not mature enough visually to maintain efficient visual skills during long periods requiring near-point vision. This child may be given visual exercises or his near-vision tasks may be broken into short segments by the teacher. In any case, if problems are evident then the school should be informed and the child should be referred for a complete vision examination.

In some cases actual vision problems exist, making difficult the use of two eyes simultaneously and causing the child to make compensation. In the medical clinics and schools the use of the Snellen Chart is a common procedure. While this is good for general vision screening, it does not tell us how the child is able to use his eyes in near-vision tasks. Thus, it is important to also check near-point vision. Schoolwork is almost all the near-vision type. Thus, a child may perform well at 20 feet away where convergence and linear tracking do not create a great deal of stress on the eyes and are at a minimum, yet on near-vision tasks the child will have difficulty. The Snellen Chart, which makes use of the E in various positions, also creates problems for children who have directional difficulties although they may have no real vision difficulty. There are vision tests available that require little or no verbalization or refined directional skills, and these should be used with children who are suspected of having some sort of problem in these areas.

Drawing Tests

Within the perceptual motor area, drawing tests are used extensively both in clinics and in school as a measure of school readiness or for determining difficulties relative to fine motor and perceptual abilities. Aside from the perceptual motor aspects of drawing and writing skills, examiners often make emotional or personality inferences from various drawing tests. Some professionals use various test instruments that use the drawings of a child to gain some idea about intelligence. In both personality and intelligence testing much training and skill are required to make accurate conclusions about intelligence and personality, and in general these inferences should not be attempted in a screening program such as the one outlined in this book. Some aspects of personality and intelligence will be observed generally during the testing. However, actual inferences about intelligence and personality from the drawing tests included in this battery should be made cautiously.

Form Copying and Drawing Testing

In most drawing tests involving forms, the child is presented with one or several stimulus pictures, which he is to copy using freehand techniques. The Bender Gestalt for children, listed as a supplementary test, is perhaps one of the most widely used by psychologists and also for general screening in clinics. It can be mastered by the mental health professional and can provide indicators of organicity, personality, and emotional maturity. Yet, the skill required for this sort of interpretation is extensive. Conversely, the Bender Gestalt can be used in a general way as a screening device for perceptual growth. The examiner who wishes to explore this test should not do so until other tests have been mastered and until some sophistication in their use is gained. Even with practice, however, this instrument will not provide the in-depth interpretations that might be made by a professional psychologist. For the purposes of this screening battery it is recommended that the Berry Test of Visual Motor Integration be used as part of the primary battery. The Berry provides age norms for children two and one half years through fifteen years and, therefore, is a good general screening test to determine general fine motor perceptual development. It also provides indicators for children as young as eight months through three years for which no specific norms are used. Thus, it is an extremely useful instrument for the examiner. The test involves having the child copy a number of forms, beginning with simple lines and proceeding to very complex forms and combinations of forms.

The Berry is inexpensive and includes a special form sheet for use by the child. The Berry also includes, in the back of the manual, some recommendations for remediation of specific difficulties in fine motor skills, which are helpful to the parents and teachers.

There are several developmental behaviors that should be noted by the examiner as the child accomplishes the drawings. The drawings themselves can be scored without seeing the child do them, but performance during the testing is as critical as the actual work produced. Watching the child work can verify or nullify many suspicions aroused during the early screening tasks.

The authors have found that use of the drawing sheets provided with the test tends to prevent observations of some critical behaviors. The examiner may wish to use the forms initially, but experience suggests that giving the child one to three sheets of paper on which he can draw all of the forms is preferred. The commercial sheets have specific places for three forms to be drawn on each sheet. This confines and directs the child's general spatial organization. It is useful to have the child simply begin with a sheet of paper and instruct him to draw the forms as they are presented to him. The child is told there will be several forms, and he is to draw them on the piece of paper. Younger children will tend to draw large forms and will need several sheets of paper. Children seven years and older will usually draw all of the forms on one sheet. This allows for many observations not possible in the usual administration of the test. Figures 1 through 6 are reproductions of children's drawings of some of the Berry forms. Aside from scoring the forms according to the Berry directions, which will yield a general visual-motor age equivalent, the following aspects of test behavior should be observed as indicators of potential visual-motor difficulties.

1. *General organization of the forms on the paper*

The child who is over six years old will usually organize the forms in a left-to-right fashion on the page. The younger the child the fewer the number of forms on each line, but children will usually organize them from left to right in rows down the page (see Figure 1).

Children who are immature, who have great difficulties with making the forms, who have spatial organization difficulties, and who cannot attend to general organization, all tend to avoid or unwittingly produce the forms in random placement all over the page (see Figure 2).

This is a good point at which to explain another ability or skill that comes with maturity. Spatial relations and spatial organization are a consequence of good perceptual motor development and learning. Most children learn to organize their space in a left-to-right fashion and from top to bottom, as this is taught in

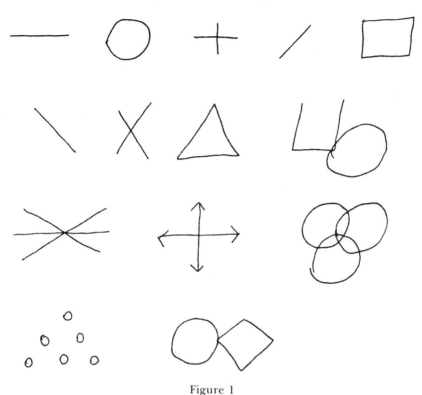

Figure 1

school and represents the way learning materials are organized. The child who is immature motorically, while he may be aware of spatial organization and the proper way to organize, will not "think" of spatial relationships due to his need to focus his attention solely on the task, which is, motorically, too difficult for him. Thus, spatial organization is important, and any deviance from it during the task is an important indicator of perceptual-spatial difficulty. This child will often be the same one whose written work at school is random and sloppy. The teacher often does not realize this is not merely a lack of attention but rather a lack of maturity and readiness for tasks that are being presented. Since the child does not attend to spatial relationships, he will often space his letters poorly on the page, along with some being large and others being small.

Figure 2

Figure 3

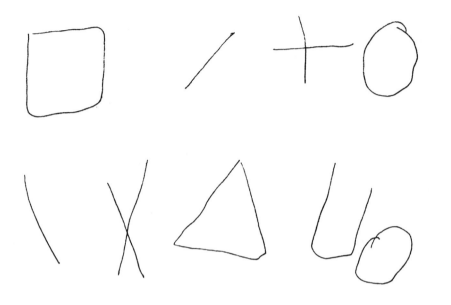

Figure 4

Children with directional difficulties often avoid the issue of organizing left to right by drawing each form and organizing them in a vertical pattern down the page. This does not happen frequently, but when it does it most often indicates poor directional organization (see Figure 3).

Left-handed children and those with directional confusion will sometimes organize the forms from right to left on the page. These children may proceed from right to left on one line and on the next reverse the direction. They are uncertain as to the correct direction and so they simply organize whichever way seems most appropriate at the moment. This should be noted along with other directional confusion indicators (see Figure 4).

2. *Diagonal and directional confusion*

Children who have developed good spatial organization or integrated the movements in various directions may tend to distort the forms in specific ways. Often in forms made with diagonal lines they will have difficulty with the angles, resulting in rounded edges on triangles and diamonds. This is usually

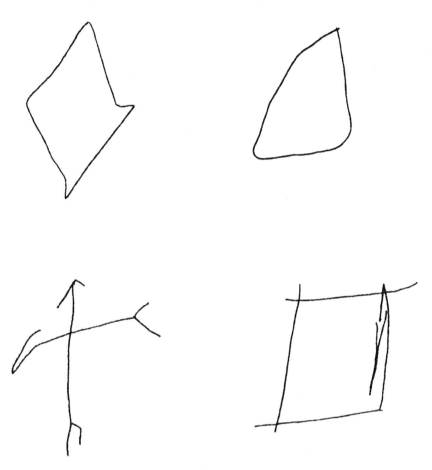

Figure 5

fairly obvious. These children often have poorly integrated movements and make their squares by drawing four lines that meet each other rather than making one continuous line into a square. Also, these children may draw the diagonal lines in the wrong direction, running from top left to bottom right, and vice versa. Other children with directional and diagonal difficulties will put tails on their diamonds, triangles, and on the form requiring the making of two crossed arrows. The arrowheads will often be drawn in the opposite direction. Examples of these problems are shown in Figure 5.

3. *Erasures*

Children who are having difficulty with directional movements, angles, and spatial arrangements often are bright enough to recognize that their productions are inaccurate. They will often erase frequently and finally give up, having produced only poorly made forms. These children are intellectually competent but are encountering great difficulties with fine motor and spatial development. They often become quite frustrated because they know that their work is inaccurate. In school these children have great difficulty in writing, and their papers are marred by many erasures. Again, often the teacher feels they are not trying hard enough or are simply inattentive when, in fact, they have not matured enough or had enough practice to complete the tasks required of them. This is a very common problem and one that, too often, teachers do not understand. Such children need much more fine motor practice, and when this practice is not allowed, the children continue to have new skills presented to them but without time to practice them. As they proceed ahead they become more and more frustrated and may appear hyperactive or become behavior problems. The alert examiner, understanding this difficulty, can often assist the school in making the proper adjustments to assist these children.

One point should be made here about the responsibilities of the examiner. The screening developmental examination is intended to identify developmental difficulties. However, it is not the responsibility of the mental health professional to attempt to tell educators how best to teach children. Once the professional teacher is alerted to a child's needs, he or she should be expected to develop remediation. The screening program is intended to pinpoint areas of need for children, but when the needs require educational intervention, it is the school's responsibility to develop that intervention.

4. *Size and general proportion*

The size of various drawings that the child is copying should meet two general criteria; they should approximate the size of the stimulus models, and they should vary as the result of pre-planning relative to space available on the page. Generally again, children under the age of six years will sometimes make the drawing larger than the models and may even use one sheet of regular 8½ by 11 inch paper for each drawing. This is unusual, but it does indicate immaturity in fine motor movements. After the age of six years most children will place at least three forms on each sheet of paper and in most cases will draw the majority of forms on one sheet. Consistency in size is important, and most normal children will make all of the forms a fairly consistent size. Variations in the extreme between the size variation forms also indicate possible immaturity and poor fine motor control. In the case of drawings in which there are two or more forms, the various integrated forms should be somewhat similar in size. Some children display emotional indicators during the drawing of forms, which are important for the examiner to note. These indicators are not totally valid and must be interpreted cautiously by the examiner. For example, withdrawn or anxious children, attempting to do the correct thing, will overcontrol and make the forms very small. This sometimes indicates emotional and perceptual constrictions and possible anxiety about the testing (see Figure 6). The examiner should verify such tendencies by watching the child's general behavior and his performance on other items of the testing. Some anxious children will make many erasures even though their forms are essentially acceptable. In this case the child may be attempting perfection because of self-perceived needs to satisfy the examiner. This can

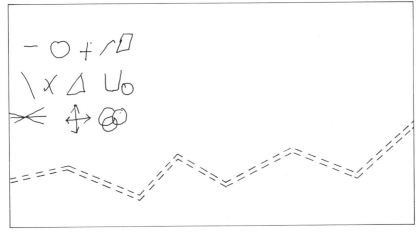

Figure 6

be caused by anxiety about self-acceptance. In some cases children will make all of the forms on one side of the paper — either left or right — which can be an indicator of preference for one side of the visual field or potential neurological difficulties in the neglected side. Again, this is a difficult factor to evaluate from drawings only, and other indicators should be taken into account during evaluation. Such indicators should be presented during the meeting of the staff concerning the child at a later time.

It should be noted that how the child produces the forms is as important as the skill with which he completes them. This is why the examiner should always watch and encourage the child. In the following section on person drawing, additional comments are made concerning how a child produces various drawings.

Draw-A-Person

An extremely important evaluation used with children to assess both personality and perceptual maturity is that of asking the child to draw a person freehand. Again, the skilled psychologist can derive many kinds of information from person drawings, which the mental health professional will need to be somewhat conservative about. General emotional indicators and perceptual factors can be discovered by the examiner, but inferences should be limited to general observations and not to indepth psychological inferences. Difficulties that are noted should be verified during other aspects of testing. This function of veryifying various observations through different tests is an important aspect of the total evaluation.

The draw-a-person activity is primarily used as a perceptual-motor and conceptual developmental tool in the psychometric screening program. The DAP or Draw-A-Person Test is sensitive to many aspects of personality and, when used by a trained psychologist, can give many projective forms of information. Such interpretation should be given only by a trained individual; therefore, the criteria here are primarily those developmental differences in general coordination and self-awareness that will affect the child's responses. We refer to this evaluation as simply a draw-a-person activity rather than labeling it the DAP for these reasons.

The child is given a piece of 8½ by 11 inch paper and simply asked to draw a person. It is often important to tell children who are eight years or older that we are interested not so much in how well they can draw as how they have learned to draw. This often puts anxious children somewhat at ease. Most children will draw a person about 60 to 70 percent as large as the paper, leaving room around the sides and the top and the bottom. The child should be given as long as he requires to make the drawing. If the child asks specific questions, such as what sex, how large, and so forth, the examiner simply replies that he should draw whatever sort of person he wants, but it would be better if he tries to draw a whole person rather than a stick figure. The following criteria should be noted about the drawing and how the child draws.

1. *Size*

It has been mentioned that most children will draw a person about 60 percent the size of the paper. Less mature children may draw the figure larger and with much more simplicity than more mature children. Further, when the drawing varies either toward larger or smaller than 60 percent, the examiner should note this.

2. *Body parts and proportions*

One of the perceptual-motor characteristics that is important in this test is to see if the child draws all of the major body parts. The child between three and six years of age may often leave out specific body parts. This often suggests a lack of internal awareness and sophistication in both body awareness and maturity. The child who is older than six years who leaves off arms or legs, who omits the torso, the neck, or other important features may be somewhat immature in general body awareness and subsequent general conceptual awareness. To draw all of the major parts, the child has to be aware of his own body concept, and he has to visualize this internally before placing it on the paper. The immature child may expend much effort on the drawing and become so absorbed in specific aspects that he forgets to complete important parts. This sort of immaturity is important to note. The drawing should display generally appropriate proportions to various body parts. Legs should not be overly long, hands or feet should not be overly large or very small, and the proportions of head, body, and legs should be more or less appropriate.

3. *Elaboration and detail*

Elaboration and detail on the drawing suggest higher levels of maturity, higher intelligence, creativity, artistic ability, and more sensitivity. The usual body parts should include —

a. Head, torso, legs, and arms;
b. Neck, hands, feet, and waist;
c. Eyes, hair, fingers, ears, and toes;
d. Dress.

Elaborations and detail often include —

a. Pupils, eyebrows, and facial characteristics;
b. Belt, necklace, wristwatch, and other specific accessories;
c. Toys, dogs, trees, and other objects;
d. Movement and activity;
e. Special emotional expression;
f. Stylized drawings of special friends and heroes.

In Goodenough's Draw-A-Man Test there are specific numbers of points given to such elaborations, which assist in gaining an estimate of a child's intelligence. Reference to that test is given in the supplementary tests listed at the end of the chapter.

4. *Drawing methods*

Some children will draw the figure from the bottom up, but most children draw from the top down. While many personality factors are attributed to this difference in method, the authors have found that children with directional problems, who are left-handed, and who generally are poorly developed motorically will often draw from the bottom up. A major reason for this is that the child has difficulty with space and does not know where to stop. By beginning at the bottom he has a concrete basis for working the figure. This suggests a degree of immaturity or perceptual motor difficulty, and should be noted.

Most children will press appropriately with the pencil, but some will draw very lightly and others with a very heavy stroke. Children with difficulties in fine motor coordination may go either way, and either should be noted. Children with perceptual or fine motor difficulties may also draw the figure so that it appears to be falling down or floating. Again, this may indicate poor spatial and directional orientation and should be noted. Children with developmental difficulties may also take a long time, or they may make a very simple drawing attempting to "get it over with" as soon as possible. The examiner should be very sensitive to the emotional mood and responsivity of the child during the activity to estimate if the child is truly involved and demonstrates willingness to complete a good drawing.

The authors have found that it is often advantageous to have the child make up his own drawing at a later time in the session. In this case the child is given some crayons and asked to draw a picture of whatever he wants and color it. Sometimes a child who is uncertain or who is resisting will draw a very different drawing

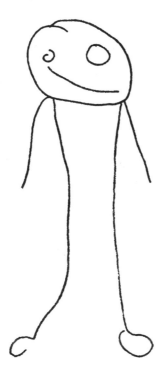

Figure 7. Age 4.6.

Figure 8. Age 5.5.

Figure 9. Age 7.5.

Figure 10. Age 8.9.

Figure 11. Age 11.

SCREENING PROFILE
DEVELOPMENTAL ASSESSMENT
PERCEPTUAL MOTOR INDICATORS   Date of Assessment_____

Name_____Age_____Birthdate_____

Parent's name_____Phone_____

Address_____Zip_____

School attending_____Grade_____

General Physiological factors:

Size: _____

General appearance:_____

Attitude:_____

General movement:_____

Dress:_____

	Poor 1 2 3	Adequate 4 5 6	Excellent 7 8 9
1. Balance on one foot with eyes open.........	_ _ _	_ _ _	_ _ _
2. Balance on one foot with eyes closed.......	_ _ _	_ _ _	_ _ _

3. Major foot used Right___Left___

4. Dominant eye Right___Left___Neither___

| 5. Ear-hand cross lateral..................... | _ _ _ | _ _ _ | _ _ _ |

6. Angels in the snow

a. Verbal directions................	_ _ _	_ _ _	_ _ _
b. Visual directions................	_ _ _	_ _ _	_ _ _
c. Kinesthetic directions...........	_ _ _	_ _ _	_ _ _

7. Visual skills

a. Tracking horizontally............	_ _ _	_ _ _	_ _ _
b. Tracking vertically..............	_ _ _	_ _ _	_ __
c. Tracking diagonally..............	_ _ _	_ _ _	_ _ _
d. Convergence......................	_ _ _	_ _ _	_ _ _

8. Form Copying

a. General organization.............	_ _ _	_ __	_ _ _
b. Size and directional orientation...	_ _ _	_ _ _	_ _ _
c. Execution........................	_ _ _	_ _ _	_ _ _
d. General quality..................	_ _ _	_ _ _	_ _ _

9. Draw-a-Person

a. Size.............................	_ _ _	_ _ _	_ _ _
b. Proportion.......................	_ _ _	_ _ _	_ _ _
c. Elaborations.....................	_ _ _	_ _ _	_ _ _
d. Execution........................	_ _ _	_ _ _	_ _ _
e. General Quality..................	_ _ _	_ _ _	_ _ _

Figure 12. Screening Assessment.

when allowed to make up his own. Further, this allows some additional indicators concerning colors, type of drawing, and general motivation, which cannot be found by asking the child to draw what you want him to.

5. *Scoring and evaluation of the perceptual motor section*

A general guideline is given on page 92 for scoring the efforts of the child. Because this is not an in-depth evaluation but rather a screening assessment, general scoring along with much observational data is the best approach. This information is then provided for the team, and appropriate further tests or recommendations can be made at that point. The main purpose of the screening assessment is to gain structured information about a child, which can lay the basis for a meeting of all persons involved with evaluating and meeting the needs of the child.

Test References

1. *Perdue Perceptual Motor Survey* – A Test of Visual Motor Abilities
   Charles Merrill Publishing Company
   1300 Alum Creek Dr.
   Columbus, Ohio 43216
2. *Frostig's Test of Visual Perception*
   Consulting Psychologists Press
   577 College Ave.
   Palo Alto, California 94306
3. *The Berry Developmental Test of Visual Motor Integration*
   Follett Publishing Company
   P. O. Box 5705
   Chicago, Illinois 60680
4. *The Draw-A-Person: A Catalogue for Interpretive Analysis,* Urban, W. 1963
   Western Psychological Services
   Box 775
   Beverly Hills, California 90213
5. *The Bender Visual Motor Gestalt Test for Children,* Clawson, Aileen
   Western Psychological Services
   Box 775
   Beverly Hills, California 90213

Chapter 6

LEARNING SKILLS ASSESSMENT

THE ASSESSMENT of skills in children and adolescents is an important area of screening for the mental health professional as well as the teacher. In the authors' clinical work most of the children and adolescents referred due to some emotional or behavioral problem exhibit some degree of difficulty in educational skills. The child with behavioral problems has often suffered educationally, and in many cases the lack of adequate learning skills has been primary to the emotional deficit. Certainly, children who have not done well in school have found much frustration resulting in adjustment difficulties. Many children who are experiencing some sort of emotional or family crisis, though they have no learning difficulties, may temporarily display lowered production in school. This sort of difficulty will usually be indicated during the initial interview with the parents. Our concern in this chapter is that if the parents do report poor school achievement, the mental health professional will be able to assess the child's learning skills.

In the preceding chapter the assessment of perceptual-motor development was discussed, and reference will be made here to basic perceptual-motor skills as related to learning. Children who display difficulties in basic perceptual-motor development will often find basic learning tasks difficult. When the mental health professional or teacher notes some difficulty in perceptual-motor functioning, he should be alert to how these may relate to specific learning problems. The following examples illustrate some relationships that may be seen:

Perceptual-Motor Deficit	*Possible Educational Consequence*
1. Poor balance and kinesthetic function	..... Difficulty producing letters, frequent reversals, confusion in sequencing, spelling errors,

94

clumsiness, general disorgani-
zation, and forgetfulness

2. Lack of established
   hand dominance .... Poor handwriting and poor
   spatial organization

3. Directional confusion .... Whole-word substitutions in
   reading, poor phonetic ability,
   reversals in writing and reading,
   difficulty in sports or any activity requiring eye-hand coordination

4. Poor visual skills .... Inability to concentrate during
   reading and writing activities,
   restlessness during seatwork,
   gross distortions in writing and
   fine motor work, loses place
   frequently when reading

These few examples illustrate some of the general relationships that exist between specific perceptual-motor difficulties
and learning skills. Many children brought to the clinic for
behavioral problems exhibit both perceptual-motor problems
and learning deficits. It is important to know something of a
child's general achievement and learning development in the
total overview of his person. To assume that a child who is
displaying emotional or behavioral difficulties has only some
sort of intrapsychic disorder is to be naive about how complex
the human mind can be. It has been our experience that prior to
making assumptions about the underlying difficulties creating a
behavioral disorder, a complete read out of the child's general
integrities must be ascertained. In too many cases a child may be
diagnosed as having the difficulties that the diagnostician is most
comfortable and experienced in recognizing. As diagnosticians,
we all have our special interests, our area of expertise, and if we
are not careful, diagnosis can be a process of merely confirming
our own biases. Thus, within the holistic mental health construct,
we must attempt to gain an initial overview of the child's assets
and liabilities throughout various areas of behavioral function-

ing. In this way we receive information that pinpoints a difficulty from several viewpoints. It is not that the mental health specialist should be expected to be competent in all areas of human behavior, but rather that a general screening be accomplished to fully describe the child's multiplex system of internal functioning.

Reading Difficulties

Assessment of reading difficulties is not a complicated process, yet teachers will tell us that it is one of the most troublesome problems in teaching. Why a particular child does or does not learn to read efficiently can remain a mystery even to those highly trained in reading methodology. Yet, our concern here is not to attempt a sophisticated evaluation of reading skills; rather, the mental health worker and teacher need to ascertain a general measurement of the child's present reading skills or difficulties. More sophisticated analysis can be provided through assistance from reading specialists if the mental health worker or teacher finds a general deficit.

Assessment of reading problems, within a clinical evaluation, can be as brief as a few minutes or as lengthy as a couple of hours. Recognizing that the emotional state of the child during the evaluation can greatly affect his functioning, it is up to the diagnostician to watch for signs of resistance to the tasks. Most children, unless there is some extreme distress during testing, will make an effort adequate enough to determine general levels of skills.

During clinical evaluations there are two major areas of assessment in relation to reading, and these are usually word recognition and in many cases reading comprehension. Such an assessment yields an overall feel for the child's level of skill development but misses several major aspects of reading achievement, which must be understood by the diagnostician. The Wide Range Achievement Test (WRAT) is widely used by psychologists and mental health diagnosticians for the purpose of gaining an achievement score in word recognition, spelling, and computational math. It is recommended to the readers of this book as part of the basic assessment battery. The Wide Range Achievement Test consists of lists of words that the child is asked to identify and for which a grade equivalence is provided relative to the number of correct responses given by the child. The entire test including word recognition, spelling, and math can take less than ten minutes and provides a good overall measure of these skills.

The Peabody Individual Achievement Test (PIAT) is a more comprehensive individual test and includes not only word recognition, spelling, and math but also such areas as general information and reading comprehension. This one test can be given to children in primary through high school grades and therefore is very useful. It also is popular with psychologists but is primarily designed for teachers and counselors and can be used effectively by all mental health professionals. Thus, in a short evaluation the examiner may wish to use the WRAT, while in a more comprehensive evaluation the PIAT will be used, or in some cases, parts of the PIAT can substitute for the WRAT.

These two tests are very useful to the mental health professional and the teacher in that they are easily administered, are acceptably valid, and provide grade equivalents. These tests also have one major drawback as opposed to the more comprehensive reading assessment that might be given by a reading specialist — they do not always give a good picture of the child's "actual" reading production within the classroom setting. Certain important points must be made about "quick," individual screening tests given in a clinical setting. The following points should be kept in mind when making the reading assessment.

1. For the average or below average student there is a great difference between word recognition and reading comprehension on an individually administered test and the actual reading achievement level in the classroom.

In the classroom, reading achievement is not measured simply by how many words the child can recognize but through several other activities. In reading the child must learn not only phonetic structure and some whole words, often called sight words, but he must also accomplish pencil-paper tasks related to initial learning skills. He might have to mark letters on a worksheet, discriminating certain letters from others. He has to copy letters and find various letter combinations on individual worksheets.

The child may know all of the basic sounds and recognize all of the letters but be unable to maintain his attention on an individual assignment in the classroom. He may be having difficulty making the letters due to immaturity in the fine motor skills, or he may actually have some minor perceptual-motor difficulty that makes it difficult for him to work on paper-pencil tasks. In school, then, this child may be working on pre-primer materials or early first grade activities. Yet, on an individual test in which the child is responding directly to the examiner without paper-pencil tasks, he may be able to obtain a grade equivalent of late first grade.

As the child grows older and proceeds through the grades, the amount of individual seatwork and paper-pencil tasks increases. Thus, the child in the fourth grade may be able to recognize words at the fourth grade level but be failing reading due to poor attention span and poor paperwork. His actual reading achievement level in the classroom may be as low as late second grade even though he scores a grade equivalent of middle fourth grade on an individual reading test.

The examiner has to be alert to these problems during the evaluation and recognize that there are often great differences between the reading tasks on an actual reading test and those of actual application in the classroom. During other aspects of the achievement evaluation the examiner will be able to see indicators of this difference.

2. Visual deficits, fine motor difficulties, and motivational difficulties can intervene in effective reading skill development even though the child exhibits adequate recognition and comprehension.

Children who have trouble with visual fixation, visual tracking, and binocularity, though they have adequate reading skills, will have difficulty maintaining attention long enough to do well on reading and writing tasks in school. When given a brief screening test, these children will be able to display their skills, but in the classroom where a longer span of attention and effort is required, they break down early and cannot complete their assignments.

To recognize these problems requires that the examiner give more than just the WRAT or the PIAT as measures of reading achievement. If a child does adequately well on these tests, yet there is a report of poor school achievement, then some endurance testing must be done. This can be accomplished easily through the use of reading paragraphs. The examiner should have reading paragraphs from each grade level, which the child is asked to read aloud, giving the examiner an opportunity to assess additional aspects of reading. Reading paragraphs for this purpose are given at the end of this chapter along with some word recognition tasks. The child is asked to read the paragraph that is appropriate for the level of word recognition attained on either the WRAT or the PIAT. The examiner should watch for the following reading errors, which can indicate visual and endurance difficulties.

a. Frequent loss of place;
b. Difficulty moving the eyes from the end of one line to the beginning of the next line;
c. Omission of words;
d. Substitution of one word for another;
e. Poor fluency in reading;
f. Adequate reading initially and then an obvious increase in the foregoing errors.

After the administration of a quick-scoring reading test such as the WRAT or the word lists at the end of the chapter, the child should be given the PIAT or the reading paragraphs at the end of the chapter. The child should be able to achieve roughly an 80 percent level of recognition on a paragraph to demonstrate adequate reading skills at that level. The comprehension questions on the PIAT can be more easily scored than the individual reading paragraphs; however, the individual reading paragraphs will provide information not available through the use of the PIAT.

The PIAT presents short sentences and paragraphs. The child is asked to read one and is then given four pictures that illustrate what was said in the paragraph. The child picks the one he feels best represents the meaning of the paragraph. Because the child does not have to respond verbally, an important area with which the child may have difficulty is neglected.

The examiner may choose to use one or the other of these methods of testing with a particular child while in another case he may choose to use both. The following will clarify the choices. When a child reads a paragraph from the PIAT he performs the following skills:

1. The child reads the paragraph aloud, giving the examiner an opportunity to check for fluency, proper intonation, and pauses, and whether the child reads word-by-word or in continuous thoughts.
2. The child selects one of four pictures, which best explains the paragraph. Although this permits guessing, it also permits those children who do not have adequate language skills to express their thoughts and in this way communicate their ability to comprehend what they have read. It is important to remember that the child with poor language skills may be required to express himself verbally in the classroom; therefore, he may do well on this test and poorly at school.

When a child reads a paragraph such as those given at the end of this chapter, he exhibits the following skills:

1. The child reads the paragraph, giving the examiner the opportunity to evaluate the same skills as on the PIAT. The passage is somewhat longer than the paragraph on the PIAT, giving the examiner the opportunity to see if the child can maintain adequate reading skills over a longer period of time as well as whether there is a consistent pattern to the errors made.
2. The child relates the meaning of the paragraph to the examiner. This enables the examiner to evaluate if the child displays continuity in thought, is capable of organizing what he has read into a verbal response, and if he is able to report it.

Thus, in reading the paragraph on the PIAT, the child is able to recognize a response instead of creating one. This means that the child may be able to achieve a higher reading-comprehension score on the PIAT than he is able to demonstrate in the classroom. The examiner must, therefore, recognize that tests like the PIAT, though they provide a quick-scoring, easily administered test, often generate a higher score and do not give a true picture of the child's actual classroom achievement level. This should be considered by the examiner when making judgments about the child's achievement skills in an examination setting as opposed to actual application in the classroom.

Determining Reading Expectation Levels

It is very important to determine an expectation for a child's reading level. For example, if Billy comes to the examiner in January, the middle of his fourth grade year, it might be felt that he is reading adequately if he is reading at the mid-fourth grade level. This may be true or it may be far from the case. In Billy's case it is not true. Billy is nine years old and started school at the appropriate age of six, though he had just turned six a few days prior to the cut-off date for school entrance. Billy is at least six months younger than the majority of the children in the fourth grade class, yet he is reading on a mid-fourth grade level. This implies two things; he is brighter than the average child his *age*, and he has done well in school. He is reading *above* level for his age, at grade level for the number of years he has been in school, and appropriately for a child with an IQ of slightly above average. The intelligence score, as an indicator of mental *age*, means that we would expect a child who is brighter to be more likely to handle an advanced reading level for his age. The data are as follows:

Case A

Present Date: January 12, 1978
Birthdate: September 3, 1968
Chronological Age: 9 years 4 months
Grade Placement: 4.4
Reading Level: 4.4
Expected Reading Level for Age: 4.4
Intelligence Score: 115
Mental Age: 10.6
Reading Expectancy for Mental Age: 5.6

The complete information of this case gives a different perspective than when we simply look at actual age and grade placement in school. There is no problem for Billy in that he is learning at the appropriate level for the amount of instruction he has received. Even though he began school at an age six months younger than most of his classmates, he is doing all right. Yet, he is performing at a reading level 1.2 years below reading expectance for a child with his mental age. Nothing would be done in this case in that his achievement is appropriate for his grade placement. It does seem important, however, for the teacher to realize that expectations for him in school should be somewhat beyond his present level of achievement. Whether or not the teacher places more expectations on him relative to his actual mental-age expectancy depends on a number of factors. It is important for the diagnostician to realize that school achievement is a complex issue and grade placement, mental age, achievement, and expectancy levels must be considered rather than simply looking at reading level. In most cases, it is appropriate to place expectancy on the basis of *mental age and achievement,* and not on grade placement and/or chronological age. Let us examine another case.

Case B

Date: September 1, 1978
Birthdate: July 1, 1968
Chronological Age: 10 years 2 months
Grade Placement: 5.1
Reading Level: 3.5

In this case it would appear that the child is nearly one and a half years behind in reading. He is ten years old, the appropriate age for being a fifth grader. He has been in school for five years and should be at a 5.1 reading level; but should he? What about his mental age? We have had parents come to the clinic upset with the school because they were not doing an effective job of teaching with such a child. Look at the rest of the data.

Mental Age: 8.4
Intelligence Score: 85
Reading Expectancy for Mental Age: 3.4

In this case the school has apparently been doing a good job, for though he has been in school for five years, his mental age tells us that he should be reading at a middle third grade reading level. Even though he is in the fifth grade and is ten years old, we should expect only that level of reading which is appropriate for his mental age, which is 8.4. Suppose that we found that his mental age was 12.10 with an intelligence score of 125. Now the expectation would change to a seventh grade level, and he is actually more than two years behind the expectancy for his mental age.

These two cases illustrate the need for the diagnostician to obtain a mental age, chronological age, grade placement, years in school, and other data if he is to truly understand the child's achievement pattern. For some children their underachievement, relative to their mental age, may have no effect on school placement. Yet, other children who are seemingly appropriately placed may be underachieving or overachieving depending upon all of these factors.

The diagnostician should be able to obtain the foregoing data. This, whether you are a teacher, a social worker, a mental health professional, or any number of other individuals who work with children, should be done so as to understand the child's needs and set appropriate expectations. Expecting the child in Case B to read at the fifth-grade level is inappropriate, and without all of the information both the teacher and parent could create a failure syndrome or worse, emotional problems.

The diagnostician, then, should have available such tests as the Slossen and the Peabody Picture Vocabulary Test to obtain a rough estimate of mental age. There should be both word-recognition and comprehension tests such as the WRAT and the PIAT available. A good history of the child's school and learning experiences should be included.

Handwriting and Spelling

Some children, though they can read adequately, may do poorly in school due to poor writing skills. Handwriting has become less important both in school and in our occupations. Machines are doing our work for us. Yet, writing is more than a means of filling out employment forms or writing a letter. Writing is a critical process in the exercise of learning information. The child who has to write a report, take notes in class, take a spelling test, or copy information in the classroom is dependent upon adequate handwriting skills.

Good handwriting, like any skill, involves certain basic functions that produce a response with the least effort and highest efficiency. Writing is a means of getting our thoughts on paper, and though the writing need not be perfect, it should involve a nonconscious and effortless activity so that it does not detract from what we are communicating. *How* we write should be automatic while *what* we write is produced with conscious awareness of our thoughts.

Thus, the goal is not to write perfectly but to write efficiently. Efficiency requires appropriate strokes and movements producing attractive and readable words. It is not beauty that we are after, but without attractiveness our writing is difficult to read and detracts from our thoughts. Handwriting must be practiced, and that is not done enough in most of today's schools. An individual may be very bright verbally, do well in reading, and fail in school because of poor writing skills. The teacher cannot assess achievement unless the child can demonstrate his knowledge. In the primary grades there is a great deal of verbal interaction between the teacher and the student, but in higher grades the teacher must have written proof of the child's knowledge. If the child cannot write, what he knows will be of little value because the teacher will not have written proof of that knowledge. It is important then to evaluate the child's ability to write during an assessment of school achievement. Assessment of the child's writing skills, in the general diagnosis, is not one of depth and detail as might be used by the teacher who is developing the child's handwriting skills. Rather, the diagnostician needs some general assessment of the skills in handwriting that the child presently possesses.

Two ways in which the diagnostician can obtain a general feel for the child's handwriting skill are through the copying of sentences, words, or paragraphs, or through a brief spelling test. There are two levels of interest in the handwriting and spelling survey — how the child makes his letters, the more mechanical aspect of his effort, when copying information, and the consistency of the handwriting pattern when he is taking dictation. The following activities can be used for this purpose.

General Handwriting Assessment

The diagnostician should use a copying task for the child that is appropriate to his achievement or grade level. This can be done most easily by having him copy, either in cursive or manuscript, a sentence or paragraph from the reading test. The handwriting task should require at least three to five minutes of effort so that fatigue factors can be noted. Thus, it must not be too long or too short. The appropriate task would be to ask the child to copy sentences from the highest level that he can read on the PIAT or the reading paragraphs listed at the end of the chapter.

Spelling Assessment

The WRAT and the Slossen Intelligence Test include spelling tests, and these can be used by the diagnostician to obtain both an analysis of errors and an actual grade equivalent. If these two tests are not being used, then words from the reading vocabulary can be used simply to check errors. At least five words should be used for primary-level students and up to at least ten words for secondary students. Aside from gaining a grade equivalent for spelling and math from the WRAT and PIAT, other specific learning functions should also be observed both during the testing and after the work is finished. The following factors should be observed:

Handwriting Characteristics

1. *Automation* — as the child is copying a sentence or paragraph, the diagnostician should observe how the child is copying. Children who have good handwriting skills will tend to write at least one word before looking back at the model. Other children will write the entire sentence. Many children who have not developed adequate writing skills will not be able to write without checking each letter. This becomes a habit with children who have difficulty making the letters in the primary grades. They are uncertain of the

structure of each letter and develop the habit of looking at each letter as they copy it. In this way they are simply copying a series of individual letters and never gain a total perceptual awareness of the word they are copying. Some children can be asked to relate what the sentence said after they are finished, and they will be unable to report it because they copied a series of letters without ever being aware of the words or their meaning. The child who does this could just as well be copying nonsense symbols. Such a child will need to be taught to look at the whole word before copying it and to increase his visual memory span.

2. *Consistent form, spacing, and organization* — Based on adequate spatial and sensory-motor skills, the child should be able to make the letters with fairly consistent form. Children with difficulties in writing have problems controlling their movements — the same letter will seldom appear to have been made as a result of the same movement. Jerky strokes, poorly executed movements, varying size, shape, and space relationships all demonstrate inadequate and inefficient writing skills.

3. *Proportion of letters, slant, and symmetry* — An additional factor in evaluating writing is the proportionate size of one letter to another. Many children with visual problems in discrimination, memory, and recognition are unable to accurately proportion the size of one letter to another. Maintaining good slant and/or vertical and horizontal relationships is also a problem with many children and decreases both their skill level and their productivity. Symmetry is the outcome of adequate skill and practice. Many children learn to make the letters and can do well except that their writing tends to be sloppy. In most cases sloppy writing is the result of difficulties in all of these areas. The difficulties are primarily a lack of adequate visual, motor, and integrative functions, which are poorly developed due to a lack of opportunity and practice. Writing does take practice, and too often there is not enough time in school for this sort of activity.

Spelling Errors

One of the major errors to look for in spelling, beyond that of merely being unable to spell, is that of the mechanics of writing and perceptual errors that are made by the child even though he is able to spell the word. Some children will exhibit good writing skills when they are copying but have great difficulty when taking dictation. For these children, the skill of writing has not become automatic, so that when they are thinking about spelling the word they forget about the letter formation, and if they think about the letter formation, spelling becomes a real problem. The following are errors related to perceptual difficulties and poor learning habits.

1. *Reversals in the order of the letters and letter omissions* — Children who have poor writing, who must concentrate on the structure of the word instead of its content, often make mistakes. They must constantly shift their attention from content — internal language imagery of how the word is spelled — to structure of the letters. When making this perceptual shift they may omit letters or reverse the sequence of the letters. Words that are misspelled due to the reversals in letter order or have a letter omitted should be correlated with the child's general writing proficiency and with any potential motor difficulties that may have been discovered.

2. *Words spelled phonetically but incorrectly* — Children who have difficulty in recalling the spelling of a whole word will often attempt to spell the word phonetically. This should be noted, for the child needs assistance in learning the whole word. Sometimes this can be due to a lack of adequate language skills, poor auditory skills, or actual hearing deficits.

3. *Sequencing errors, visual memory errors, and part-word reversals* — Some children will use all of the correct letters for a word but scramble the letters so that there are not only reversals but also various combinations of letters that illustrate phonetic errors, such as gril for girl and spilt for split. Some children will even have full reversals such as was for saw.

These sorts of errors during writing and spelling exercises should be noted. There are many specific errors that could be noted by the specialists in learning disabilities, but these few errors should be adequate for the diagnostician who is attempting to gain a good overall understanding of the child's difficulties.

The following is an achievement survey sheet that may be used as a profile summary sheet.

Achievement Survey

Name _____ Age_____ Birthdate_____

Address _____ Zip_____

Parents' Names _____ Phone _____

Grade Placement_____School_____

WRAT: Word Recognition_____Math_____Spelling_____

PIAT: Word Recognition _____ Comprehension _____ General

      Knowledge _____

      Spelling _____ Math_____

Reading Paragraphs

    Fluency _____

    Visual Endurance _____

    Tracking _____

    Inflection _____

    Phrasing _____

Writing

    Automation _____

    Consistency_____

    Spacing _____

    Organization _____

    Proportion _____

    Slant_____

    Symmetry _____

Spelling

    Reversals_____Sequencing_____Letter Omissions_____

Verbal Intelligence_____

CA _____

MA_____

Grade Placement _____
Years in School_____
Expected Reading Level_____
Actual Reading Level _____
Reading Deficit_____
Summary of Learning Difficulties and Recommendations:

Reading Paragraphs

Level I

A little boy had a dog.
The boy's dog was named Ben.
Ben was brown and white.
Ben could run fast.
The little boy ran fast too.
Ben and the little boy had fun.
Do you have a dog?
What is the name of your dog?
Can your dog run fast?

Have child read word list before reading paragraph.

Word List

1. boy	9. dog
2. ran	10. can
3. little	11. what
4. brown	12. was
5. had	13. the
6. and	14. your
7. have	15. saw
8. name	

Level II

In the old days many settlers killed buffalo for fun and not for food. Before long there were very few buffalo left in the west. Some people learned that Canada had begun to keep buffalo herds and protect them with federal laws. It was not long until the United States also began to realize that there might not be any more buffalo. Today there are great herds of buffalo in the United States and individuals also raise buffalo. Some ranchers raise buffalo just like cattle. Have you ever had a buffaloburger? Do you think this is a good idea?

1. awake
2. larger
3. dark
4. scared
5. brave
6. house
7. laugh
8. work
9. builder
10. ground
11. buffalo
12. knock
13. animals
14. battle
15. hunter

Level III

Bob's mother decided to have a garage sale on Saturday. Bob had never seen a garage sale and he said, "Mother, that seems strange. What do you sell at a garage sale?"

Bob's mother laughed. "Well Bob, we don't sell the garage. We sell things that we no longer want. That way instead of just throwing things away we can make some money. During the summer and fall seasons many people clean house and have a garage sale."

Bob was forever looking for a way to make some money so he dug around in his room. "Mom," asked Bob, "Can I sell some of these shells and this old snakeskin I bought from Joe?"

"I wonder how many people will want to buy a snakeskin, Bobby?"

He looked at her and laughed. "I guess it would be a strange thing to buy."

1. window
2. porpoise
3. clams
4. shells
5. handkerchief
6. marble
7. strange
8. empty
9. snakeskins
10. forever
11. independence
12. climate
13. season
14. garage
15. coast

Level IV

Ole Joe pulled the boat up to his dock and anchored it there with a rope. His friend racoon was always with him. Sometimes though the racoon's curiosity got him into trouble like the time that he saw an alligator in a patch of cattails. When he saw

1. hibernate
2. curiosity
3. patch
4. racoon
5. decision
6. explosion
7. unconscious
8. parachute

the alligator open his mouth he
ran so fast that he hit a tree and
nearly knocked himself unconscious. Ole Joe laughed so hard
he nearly fell off the porch of his
cabin. In all of the excitement he
did not know that the alligator,
who was also frightened,
knocked over his boat and
dumped all of his fishing
equipment into the lagoon.

9. alligator
10. turpentine
11. anchored
12. excitement
13. butterfly
14. millionaire

Ole Joe had always dreamed of
being a millionaire. He used to
sit in his boat thinking of how he
could be a great fisherman on
the ocean and catch tuna to sell
to the fishery. But he mostly just
fished in the lagoon and
watched the wildlife in the
marshes. But still he dreamed
that one day he would leave the
swamp and go out to the ocean.

Level V
Astronomers study the stars and
heavens today as they have for
thousands of years. When the
telescope was invented, many
questions that puzzled man for
centuries were solved. But as the
heavens have been more closely
examined and the location of
many stars recorded, more
questions have arisen.

1. examined
2. forecasting
3. discovered
4. centuries
5. astronomer
6. innocent
7. severely
8. disgraced
9. stampede
10. protect

Today radio telescopes are used
to pick up "noise" from the uni-
verse. Still more stars and other

11. recorded
12. require
13. establish

phenomena have been discovered. Mapping of the stars requires careful and patient effort
to establish the exact location of
all of the heavenly bodies that
are continually being added to
charts and records.

14. determined
15. opportunity

There are many opportunities
in the field of astronomy for
youth as they plan their future
careers. But the work and
training of the astronomer is
arduous. Only a small portion of
the probable bodies that exist in
the heavens have been studied.

Level VI

Many years ago scientists
warned that much of the earth's
deposit of fossil fuels would be
used up by the year 2000. There
are many politicians who campaign on platforms advocating
solving the energy problem.
The beginning of what is now
fossil fuel began in prehistoric
times as plants and animals de-
cayed and through complex
chemical processes their remains became coal. Vegetation
requires a long time to make
such a change, and none of our
computerized and electronic
marvels have produced an artificial substitute for fossil fuels. It
is not likely that in the near future they will. We have achieved
placing satellites in space but we

1. computer
2. reference
3. calculation
4. campaign
5. protein
6. capillary
7. prehistoric
8. fossil
9. chemical
10. instinct
11. deposit
12. electronic
13. atmosphere
14. satellite
15. vegetation

cannot solve our energy problem.

Test References

1. *The Wide Range Achievement Test*
   Guidance Associates of Delaware Inc.
   1526 Gilpin Ave.
   Wilmington, Delaware 19800
2. *The Peabody Picture Vocabulary Test* and *The Peabody Individual Achievement Test*
   American Guidance Service
   Circle Pines, Minnesota 55014
3. *Screening Test for Identification of Children with Specific Language Disabilities* – A series of reading related tests in the area of language processes.
   Educators Publishing Service
   75 Moulton St.
   Cambridge, Massachusetts 02138
4. *Gates-McKillop Reading Diagnostic Test*
   Teacher College Press
   1234 Amsterdam Ave.
   New York, New York 10027
5. *Durrell Analysis of Reading Difficulty*
   Harcourt Brace Jovanovich, Inc.
   757 Third Ave.
   New York, New York 10017

Chapter 7

PERSONALITY FACTORS

A SSESSMENT OF PERSONALITY is a complex and confusing field of evaluation for the teacher, counselor, or any mental health professional. Few of us are free from our biases in describing and evaluating the personality of a child or adolescent. Freudian psychological theory is quite enough of a problem for the frontline personnel who must deal with the child each day, but behaviorists and Gestalt theories do little to simplify things, and too often we are left with the need to refer the child to a clinical psychologist or psychiatrist for such assessment. Too often these routine responses, which are supposed to summarize the assessment of personality, appear on diagnostic reports:

1. The child is displaying neurotic or pre-psychotic symptoms, requiring psychotherapy.
2. The child is psychopathic, requiring a structured environment and family therapy.
3. The child is displaying primitive-unsocialized behavior, indicating a delinquency syndrome.
4. The test data display indicators of hostility, rejection, and authority-figure conflicts.
5. The child is autistic.

Such statements lend authenticity to the diagnosis but do little to assist us in understanding or structuring the child's intervention program. First of all, many of the terms listed above do not have clear definitions or symptoms that are receptive to actual intervention. Further, they are a statement of the professional's training and/or the specific tests that were used.

Conversely, we do not intend to imply that a clinical diagnosis has no purpose, for it does. However, an essential issue for the nonpsychologist or nonpsychiatrist is that practical information is not gained from much of the clinical data generated within a full-range psychological evaluation. Further, there are not enough tools available to the level-one personnel to gain an initial understanding of the child's needs and his problem. If there were more effective front-line assessment procedures, then many children would not need full-range evaluations. If more children could be screened in the environment where the problems occur, then application of intervention strategies would not only be more practical but most likely more effective.

The mental health professionals need practical ways of assessing behavior in an effort to provide immediate data. The psychologist and psychiatrist should work with those children who do not respond to such general screening. This would prevent their using valuable time to see children who could have been helped earlier.

A MENTAL HEALTH STRATEGY

The professional involved with children at the initial level of assessment needs some overall strategy or philosophy to guide his investigation. This book is intended to provide one major strategy, which should be reiterated. The assessment of a child's behavior should be initiated with an overall intention of looking at a *broad range of developmental abilities*. However, this assessment should include both assets and liabilities. In this way and only in this way can the difficulties of the child be put in proper perspective. If one aspect of the child's development is reviewed, such as learning disability or an emotional problem, the other more positive abilities may be neglected, which could alter the evaluation of the problem.

For example, a mother brought a child to the clinic with the presenting problem being that the child was having severe tantrums at home. He was five years old. There was a history of fussy behavior as an infant, parental disagreements about management and punishment, an overprotective mother, and a father who tended to be punitive and authoritarian. One could certainly make a case for the more-or-less classical rejection and intrafamily conflict as a basis for the tantrums. To some degree this was the case. More importantly, though, within the total assessment, it was found that the child was not only gifted but had poor general coordination and fine motor development. He was constantly frustrated in his attempts to do things. He could conceptualize the task but, with a lower level of motoric development, could not accomplish the task. The parents were dealing with his frustration and attempting to get him to accept their help, but they were also responding in a punitive manner to his tantrums.

Without the developmental and intellectual data, our efforts to help in this case would have been unsuccessful. The parents were well-educated people and were not impressed with their child's general level of verbal ability, for they saw it as somewhat typical and expected. The case would have been very different if the child had been average or even slightly bright, but his verbal IQ was over 160. With the initial data one could have easily drawn the conclusion that the parents were harboring much resentment for the child and that this was the primary cause of the tantrums.

Many cases of such children slip through even full-range psychological evaluations because the professional focuses on the obvious psychodynamic factors involved in the case and does not look at the relationships between all areas of development. Only after a general overview of major areas of development, both in positive and negative areas, can the most effective diagnosis be made. Thus, the first strategy is that of a full-range developmental survey of *all* children referred for any problem. Once the child has been given a total evaluation, then the presenting problems can be looked at within the context of a total viewpoint. In some cases, following the full assessment, the presenting problems are essentially related to psychodynamic factors, and other data are of little importance. Too many children are given a limited assessment, and false assumptions are made. The one child for whom seemingly unimportant information will be helpful should be reason enough to give the full assessment in every case. This brings us to the second significant data form.

The second major strategy is that of *selecting priorities* within behavioral deficits. If one only gives a psychodynamic assessment, then problems in personality and family structure may be evident and investigation can begin there. However, when a full-range assessment is given, several minor and major areas of developmental difficulties can be seen. In many cases the professional may point out several of the problems to the parents and then select two or three areas that are of greatest importance at the moment, even though there are other areas that may require attention. Once an assessment is completed, then a review of all of the data in relation to the major behavioral difficulties can yield several possibilities for intervention. It may be determined that certain areas of difficulty should be considered first while others should have less priority for a time. In other cases lower priority areas of difficulty may involve problems that will be somewhat resolved by time, i.e. developmental maturation, and some will be resolved once other, more important, areas are attended to. In that the full-range developmental assessment usually yields several areas of delayed or arrested growth, this strategy of selecting the areas of priority for intervention is very important.

The final strategy is for selection of key areas of development that are more or less important to children and adolescents. In essence, what major factors should be reviewed with all children over the age of five? The brief survey given in Chapter 4 should be used to assist in developmental assessment of children under the age of five. With school-aged children and adolescents there should be some developmental factors that come to be universally important though many specific areas are unique to particular ages only. With the lack of specificity in this general overview of development, many of the special, age-related problems are not reviewed. Thus in the remainder of this chapter our main concern is to point out some major areas of concern in the personalities of children and adolescents. Several areas will be reviewed, and the professional will have to structure his efforts from the available screening activities and instruments to fit the particular child with whom he is concerned.

GENERAL TEMPERAMENT

Temperament implies a general behavioral set that is usually somewhat distinctive to each child. Few psychologists would attempt to discuss temperament with the parents of a child. The psychologist will most often use terms such as personality or behavioral components instead. Most parents seem to understand temperament better; it has utility with parents, and more importantly, it is a viable concept that should be used by mental health professionals.

A major differentiation between temperament and what is commonly referred to as personality is that temperament can be identified soon after birth while personality is a set of behaviors that is, in fact, more vague and difficult to identify. Temperament is an identified set of behavioral factors that observably describes a child. The following factors are often used with very young children to describe temperament. We have adjusted them somewhat to be used with both children and adolescents. Once introduced to the concept of temperament, the authors have found the concept invaluable in looking at behavior and inquiring from parents about behavioral observations at home.*

1. *Activity Level* — Proportion of active periods to inactive periods.
2. *Rhythmicity* — Regularity of hunger, excretion, sleep, and wakefulness.
3. *Distractibility* — Degree to which extraneous stimuli alter behavior.
4. *Approach-Withdrawal* — Response to new object or person.
5. *Adaptability* — Ease of adapting to new environment.
6. *Attention Span and Persistence* — Period of time devoted to activity.
7. *Intensity of Reaction* — Energy of response.
8. *Threshold of Responsiveness* — Stimulus intensity required to get response.
9. *Quality of mood* — Friendly vs unfriendly behavior.
10. *Self-Modulation* — Ability to calm self following stress.

These ten behaviors can usually be evaluated by both the professional and the parents relative to school and home behavior. They are somewhat concrete behaviors, which fortu-

---

* These factors are those adapted from Thomas, A., Chess, S., and Birch, H., *Temperament and Behavioral Disorders in Children* (New York, New York University Press, 1968).

nately the parent can recall with specific behaviors in mind. The child is or is not performing in a certain manner. Thus, the temperament checklist presented here is a good way to initiate an interaction with the parents. The following interview not only yields information about the child's general temperament style, it will also add a great deal more information concerning other aspects of the child's behavior and the parent's perception of their child. The interview questions can be used as an initial interview with the parents or can be used to forward to the teacher at school.

We often use a scale of one to five or one to ten for parents and teachers, using one as very poor and three as average. Generally, one to ten works better because it gives the adult a broader range of possibilities to make discriminations. Five is average, and most parents can use such a scale easily. It really does not matter so much if the child is a four or a five, a nine or ten, or a one or two. In each case there is a tendency toward one direction or the other, and what is needed is some indication of which direction the child falls in the adult's perception. For example, many parents will say a child is a little active and report a six, indicating some degree of higher activity than other children in the family or other children they know. The child may actually be closer to a seven or even eight, but the parents may unconsciously be unwilling to indicate something they feel is negative about their child. Conversely, some parents tend to overexaggerate and might report a ten for the same child. The child may be only a six. In both cases there is an indication that the child is probably more active than most children, and with this crude measure we only want some indication of relative behavior.

Temperament Checklist

Activity Level

1. Does your child remain active during the day?   1 2 3 4 5 6 7 8 9 10
2. Does your child find things to do himself?   1 2 3 4 5 6 7 8 9 10

Rhythmicity

1. Does your child seem typically hungry during the day?   1 2 3 4 5 6 7 8 9 10

2. Does your child sleep what seems an appropriate amount of time each day and night?   1 2 3 4 5 6 7 8 9 10

Distractibility

1. Does your child seem able to concentrate adequately?   1 2 3 4 5 6 7 8 9 10
2. Does your child handle a lot of noise or activity adequately without becoming distracted?   1 2 3 4 5 6 7 8 9 10

Approach-Withdrawal

1. Does your child interact easily with other children?   1 2 3 4 5 6 7 8 9 10
2. Does your child show interest in new situations and objects or people?   1 2 3 4 5 6 7 8 9 10

Adaptability

1. Does your child adjust easily to new school settings and/or to new classrooms at the beginning of the year?   1 2 3 4 5 6 7 8 9 10
2. Does your child adjust adequately to disruptions in routine at home and school? 1 2 3 4 5 6 7 8 9 10

Attention Span and Persistence

1. Does your child follow through with projects at home and school?   1 2 3 4 5 6 7 8 9 10
2. Does your child show determination to complete projects or activities that require a large amount of committed time? 1 2 3 4 5 6 7 8 9 10

Intensity of Reaction

1. Does your child show an appropriate intensity in emotions during a crisis or personal problem?   1 2 3 4 5 6 7 8 9 10
2. Is your child able to modulate his behavior without assistance during periods of crisis?   1 2 3 4 5 6 7 8 9 10

Threshold of Responsiveness

1. Does your child appear appropriately
   alert when spoken to or asked a question? 1 2 3 4 5 6 7 8 9 10
2. Does your child pick up on humorous
   situations such as puns? 1 2 3 4 5 6 7 8 9 10

Quality of Mood

1. Is your child generally friendly and
   happy? 1 2 3 4 5 6 7 8 9 10
2. Does your child show enthusiasm for ac-
   tivities and projects he is involved in? 1 2 3 4 5 6 7 8 9 10

Self Modulation

1. Is your child able to organize his time and
   activities to fit the demands of those
   about him? 1 2 3 4 5 6 7 8 9 10
2. Does your child recover adequately following a disappointment or confrontation? 1 2 3 4 5 6 7 8 9 10

This general overview will yield a feeling for major areas of temperament style, which can give the professional much orientation about the sort of child under evaluation. Temperament is important in that it suggests not only the effects of family and environment but also prenatal and genetic factors that affect the child's behavior. Children come, as all mothers know, unique within themselves from all other children. This is not something that occurs merely from environment in that environment has not yet had its chance. However, initial birth temperament and its interaction with the environment will eventually determine personality. It is a *ratio* of the interaction of these two, rather than either nature or nurture, which is important. Environment may have the last word but its language is built upon the first blow of genetics and prenatal factors. Temperament, then, constitutes a very important factor to consider and observe as part of the total personality of the child.

LOCUS OF CONTROL

Who is in charge of the house? Hopefully, in that the house

here is in reference to the child's personality, it will be the child. From birth to approximately four or five years, most children are somewhat dependent upon the adults around them. Somewhere close to five the child begins to assert himself and establish the first level of true independence.

When a child begins to assert himself and attempts to cause others to respond to his needs and dominance, he is displaying an internal "locus of control" over his behavior. The young infant or child who is uncertain of himself yields to the direction and security provided by others about him. In this case the locus of control is the environment or is externalized. The ideal control factor is that of internal locus of control with cooperativeness and acceptance of the needs of others. Thus, internal locus of control is important in the functioning of a healthy personality. Locus of control, however, is only the first step in adequate mental health adjustment and growth. A child may be very dominant and resistive to direction by adults and peers and be an aggressive and unpleasant person to be around. With the development of a positive locus of control internally, the child must also learn and develop an understanding of the needs of others. He must learn to modulate his behavior between what he desires and the ability or need of others to accept his demands. This involves the classical problem of socialization studied by Freud and others. It is the development of an independent ego system coupled with an adequate superego structure — the compromise of personal needs and the needs of others. To be socialized in a healthy way a child has to learn to be responsible for his own behavior and to gain satisfaction through cooperative behaviors.

The concept of personal responsibility is somewhat simple in theory but very difficult in practice. Responsibility involves the individual's acceptance of the consequences of his own behavior. Responsibility also implies that one is responsible for his behavior, which gets him or denies him those responses he desires from others. This is a difficult point for most children to understand, and apparently it is not all that clear to adults either. For example, when a child or an adult desires positive attention from someone else, he seldom realizes that getting that attention is primarily his responsibility and not that of the giver. We are all so used to expecting love and attention from spouses, parents, or children that we forget that we are all individuals with similar needs. The common belief is that a mother's love is a right of the child. In practice we know that this is too often untrue. Realistically, children and adults usually have to act in loving ways to obtain love from others. To be sure, mothers will continue to give even when a child is unloving and negative, but eventually that love is given not because it is deserved but because it is a "responsibility." Responsibility without love can be a devastating thing to a child or adult. We all, children and adults, must give back to those what we expect of them; more importantly, if we want something from another we often have to give first to get. That places the responsibility on our behavioral shoulders.

Personal responsibility, then, implies that we are sensitive to the needs of others to gain our own need satisfaction. If we accept this truth then we are in control not only of ourselves but we act responsibly toward others from whom we expect or hope to gain positive rewards. Children must be taught this and not place the external control of personal responsibility on someone else.

It is important, then, that the professional establish some understanding of how well the child or adolescent is accepting personal responsibility and how adequate his internal locus of control may be. This can be observed by watching the child, but initial information must be gained from both the child and the parents or teacher. The following list of twenty questions provides a general framework within which this area can be investigated. The professional, if the opportunity presents itself in play or during testing, can use these areas as observation points or the checklist can be given to the teacher to complete along with one completed by the parents during the interview.

Locus of Control Checklist

1. Child asserts self in situations where peers attempt to dominate him? 1 2 3 4 5 6 7 8 9 10
2. Child makes requests of parents and adults for assistance or permission? 1 2 3 4 5 6 7 8 9 10
3. Child asks questions for information and/or clarification of ideas? 1 2 3 4 5 6 7 8 9 10

4. Child is able to create play activities without direction or assistance? 1 2 3 4 5 6 7 8 9 10
5. Child displays special interests and attempts to obtain approval and support for them? 1 2 3 4 5 6 7 8 9 10
6. Child attempts to influence other children in play activities to play his game? 1 2 3 4 5 6 7 8 9 10
7. Child displays appropriate assertiveness and competitive spirit? 1 2 3 4 5 6 7 8 9 10
8. Child demonstrates personalization of his room and space? (Decorates, puts up his things on walls) 1 2 3 4 5 6 7 8 9 10
9. Child demonstrates preferred ways of doing things, making things, and dressing? 1 2 3 4 5 6 7 8 9 10
10. Child shows preference in foods? 1 2 3 4 5 6 7 8 9 10

This checklist can be used with adolescents with slight alterations in the questions.

Personal Responsibility Questionnaire

1. Accepts adult supervision and limit setting? 1 2 3 4 5 6 7 8 9 10
2. Displays remorse in situations where he is reprimanded? 1 2 3 4 5 6 7 8 9 10
3. Recognizes his role in situations involving conflict? 1 2 3 4 5 6 7 8 9 10
4. Able to accept another viewpoint that differs from his own? 1 2 3 4 5 6 7 8 9 10
5. Accepts and follows through with chores, school studies, and personal hygiene? 1 2 3 4 5 6 7 8 9 10
6. Is able to display love or cooperativeness, and/or participate in situations to obtain positive responses from others? 1 2 3 4 5 6 7 8 9 10
7. Can play or interact cooperatively with other children? 1 2 3 4 5 6 7 8 9 10

8. Can understand and/or explain his behavior in situations relative to past,
present, and future?   1 2 3 4 5 6 7 8 9 10
9. Shows willingness to abide by rules of
behavior and tends to judge others who
misbehave?   1 2 3 4 5 6 7 8 9 10
10. Displays ability to organize self toward
long-range goals? (Few hours to several
weeks)   1 2 3 4 5 6 7 8 9 10

This checklist can be adapted for use with adolescents.

These areas of behavior can often be evaluated through specific personality tests, but the problem with such tests is that the information is "inferred" or projected from the questions given to the child or adolescent verbally or in written form. The same information can be obtained from three more concrete sources, the parents, observation of the child, and actual questioning of the child himself. The authors have found that children as young as five years and as old as sixteen are able to provide information if the questions are asked in language they can understand. It is extremely valuable to obtain such self-reports, for even if the child attempts to be deceptive this is significant. By observing the child, asking the parents, and interviewing the child, three points of reference and perception can be given, which provide an excellent technique for pinpointing areas of real concern. Further, if there is much disagreement between any of the parties involved, then these areas of disagreement provide a focal point for beginning discussions with the family or child.

There are two tests that can be used with elementary-school-age through adolescent-age children that give this sort of information and much more. While the techniques described here may give adequate information, many professionals often feel they need some sort of objective verification. The first test is the Devereux Behavior Rating Scale, which essentially provides a description of a child based on information from teachers, parents, and/or the professional doing the evaluation. This test, in that it is objective, can provide good verification. This test is

126   *Developmental Psychometrics*

inexpensive and can be purchased from the Devereux Foundation Press, Devon, Pennsylvania 19333. The second test, which
the authors have found extremely valuable for children and
adolescents, is the Children's Personality Questionnaire and the
16 Personality Factors for Adolescents. Both of these tests are
provided by The Institute for Personality and Ability Testing,
1602 Coronado Drive, Champaign, Illinois, and give a good
objective assessment of personality characteristics. They require
some practice but much literature is available for using these
tests. In most situations there will be a clinical psychologist or
psychometrist who can assist in the initial interpretations.

SELF-CONCEPT

Perhaps no other term has been so frequently used concerning a child who has some sort of difficulty than that of *self-concept*.
The term is usually applied to the child as a description of how he
sees himself. It is often assumed that a child's self-concept can be
"damaged," "inflated," "inadequately developed," or some other
such term, as if somewhere inside we all have a little self-concept
center, which can malfunction. Yet, we all seem to know and
agree on what we are talking about, though it is a term that can
vary tremendously from person to person relative to interpretation. Further, it seems that self-concepts can be improved by
success, by supporting a child, by assisting a child in accepting
himself, and even by acceptance by others. It would seem that
the self-concept is very vulnerable to the environmental factors
around it. We should clarify some dimensions of this issue. While
the reader may or may not agree, some definition will assist
everyone in looking at the factors that underlie self-concept.
Self-concept most basically involves a child or adult's "self-
perception," a belief, a self-imposed description of self. There
are many subtle qualities about self-perception, but in general
most of us hold some belief about ourselves. There are several
dimensions of self-concept that need to be explored. Certainly,
self-concept is a basic organizer of behavior; therefore, an estimate or understanding of a child's self-concept is a key to his own
behavioral adjustment and our assisting him in situations where
he needs help. What are some of the basic factors upon which
personal perceptions of self are developed?

1. *Physical Dimensions*
   An individual develops a personal concept based on many physical characteristics. How tall, small, heavy or thin, strong, or athletic is the individual? All of these factors can be evaluated according to social values, but here we are most concerned with the physical characteristics themselves and how the individual perceives them.

2. *Conceptual Dimensions*
   The individual has some sort of general notion about how he or she seems relative to intelligence, ability to talk, ability to understand learning or school information, solve problems, or communicate to others. There are a great range of possible factors within these areas, which contribute to self-concept. I am smart, clever, dumb, not a very good talker, a creative person, persuasive, and so forth — are all factors in the more conceptual self-concept.

3. *Affective Dimensions*
   Self-concept is also developed from one's impressions about his feelings, attitudes, and motivation. We all talk about ourselves as being a serious or joyous person, a nice person, a moody individual, a person who has to dominate, a leader, a follower, an open-minded person, a prejudiced individual, and so forth. These feelings often relate to conceptual matters, but they essentially deal with how we feel and consequently how we feel about ourselves.

4. *Social and Value Dimensions*
   A self-concept is developed from our social experience, which gives some sort of social value to our self-concept. The statements above contain many social value statements. We evaluate our behavior by the standards of our social group, and our self-concept is developed surrounding how well we are able to achieve sociability. The values of our cultural group define acceptable and unacceptable behaviors, which in turn are used to assess one's self and consequently the development of a particular self-concept.

These four dimensions of self-concept can often be observed not only in behavior of children but in what they say. During any assessment of a child's personality, some sort of assessment should be made concerning the child's perception of himself relative to these dimensions. Again, a checklist can be developed and used to sample the parents' perception of the child and the child's perception of himself. Validity of their responses is not so important as the attempt to gain additional information in another dimension of personal function. Self-concept, like temperament, is but one aspect of what we commonly refer to as the "personality" of the child. The following questionnaire can be used as a foundation with the professional adding or deleting questions as seems appropriate. New ones can be added to such an informal approach.

Self-Concept Questionnaire

Physical Dimensions

1. Is the child of the appropriate physical size (height and weight) for his age?   1 2 3 4 5 6 7 8 9 10
2. Does the child display adequate gross and fine motor coordination?   1 2 3 4 5 6 7 8 9 10
3. Is the child physically attractive?   1 2 3 4 5 6 7 8 9 10
4. Does the child display adequate stamina and endurance?   1 2 3 4 5 6 7 8 9 10
5. Is the child free of physical abnormalities and/or disorders?   1 2 3 4 5 6 7 8 9 10

Conceptual Dimensions

1. Is the child of average intellectual (verbal) ability?   1 2 3 4 5 6 7 8 9 10
2. Is the child of average creative ability? Does he display imagination, constructive skill, and mechanical ability?   1 2 3 4 5 6 7 8 9 10
3. Does the child speak and communicate adequately?   1 2 3 4 5 6 7 8 9 10
4. Is the child able to understand directions in school and at home?   1 2 3 4 5 6 7 8 9 10
5. Does the child display average learning skills?   1 2 3 4 5 6 7 8 9 10

Affective Dimensions

1. Does the child display adequate
   surgency? (A general ability to remain
   positive) 1 2 3 4 5 6 7 8 9 10
2. Is the child generally cooperative and
   courteous to others? 1 2 3 4 5 6 7 8 9 10
3. Does the child display appropriate emotional responses? 1 2 3 4 5 6 7 8 9 10
4. Is the child able to display positive feelings toward others? 1 2 3 4 5 6 7 8 9 10
5. Does the child recover easily from disappointment or frustration? 1 2 3 4 5 6 7 8 9 10

Social and Value Dimensions

1. Does the child display appropriate values
   of right and wrong? 1 2 3 4 5 6 7 8 9 10
2. Does the child recognize appropriate social behaviors in groups? 1 2 3 4 5 6 7 8 9 10
3. Does the child display adequate cooperative behaviors with others? 1 2 3 4 5 6 7 8 9 10
4. Does the child display appropriate com-
   petitive behavior and feelings of fairness? 1 2 3 4 5 6 7 8 9 10
5. Does the child display appropriate at-
   titudes toward learning goals? 1 2 3 4 5 6 7 8 9 10

These twenty factors are designed not so much to simply describe the child's behavior as they are areas in which the professional will attempt to describe self-concept. For example, "Does the child display appropriate cooperative behaviors with others?" is designed as an area of observation and interview with the child. If the child would say he feels he is cooperative, then the task becomes one of verifying his statement through behavioral observation and parent reports. If the child is not cooperative, then he must eventually be confronted with his behavior and attempts made to encourage and teach him how to be cooperative. The purpose of the questionnaire is to open up the various areas of self-concept to awareness and analysis by all parties involved with the child. In that this process is somewhat complex, several points must be made about self-concept and how to approach the analysis of this factor.

In using the self-concept questionnaire, several steps must be followed. The success of the questionnaire is not, as with many tests, dependent on the comprehensiveness or efficiency of the questionnaire, but rather dependent upon the skill of the professional in using it as a means of exploring structured areas in an open confrontation and interaction with the clients.

The questionnaire is phrased as an interview with the parents. This is the first level of use.

Phase 1

The parents should be asked each of the twenty questions, and they should give a point score to their assessment. If the questions are to be used with an adolescent, then they should be phrased with adolescent behavior in mind. Most of the questions, though, can be asked the same as if the client were an elementary child.

As the parent responds to the questions, the examiner should take notes at the margin of the paper with the following points in mind.

a. *Do the parents agree on the particular item?* If they do not then the examiner should question their difference of opinion to see if they can clarify their disagreement. In some cases it may be well to have each parent complete the questionnaire separately. After they are finished the examiner then gives each of their answers to them together and discusses them. In some cases they will each adjust their answers. Often parents will develop a more consistent awareness not only of their child but of each of their attitudes toward the child. This can be used as a means of assisting the parents in changing their behavior toward and expectations of the child.

b. *Do the parents exhibit any nonverbal behaviors?* Do the parents exhibit any nonverbal behaviors that suggest being uncomfortable with the question or their spouse's answer? If there is indication of some degree of dissonance over a question, though the parents do not state it, then this should be

brought out with "Mrs. Smith, you seem somewhat uncomfortable with this question; can you tell me about it?"

c. *Are either or both parents unable to report on a particular item?*
Why?

d. *Do the parents appear to be giving truthful responses or are there indications that they are guarded?*

Phase 2

During a second session the examiner should give the questionnaire to the child, rephrasing the questions so that the child
can answer them at his level of comprehension. Some of the
questions may be difficult for the younger children, or it may
emerge that the questions are too difficult for a child either due
to inadequate developmental maturity or defensiveness. Notes
again should be taken as to the child's behavior during the
interview. The examiner should attempt to ascertain both from
actual questions and from the child's behavior how adequate the
responses may be.

Phase 3

This phase is perhaps the most important. The questionnaire
should be forwarded to the child's teacher or another adult who
knows him well and who will probably be more objective than
either the child or the parents.

Phase 4

All three interviews are then placed on a graph, with different
colors being used to designate each of the responses. In this way
the child and the parents can see areas where the perception of
the child and adults may differ. These areas can then become
areas of therapy or instruction in which the child develops the
skills required. Most importantly, this phase allows the parents
and child to see areas where his self-concept is accurate or
inaccurate and in what specific areas the differences occur. This
gives the child concrete feedback, and his self-concept can be
improved through specifically planned activities rather than
hoping that success or acceptance from adults or peers will
somehow resolve the problem of a "poor self-concept." A poor

self-concept does not tell us much; worse, it gives us no indication of exactly how a child's self-concept is poor.

These two areas of personal organization, temperament and self-concept, with the forty questionnaire factors, provide a broad overview of practical areas of behavior that may be seen as the "personality" of the child. Some of the areas overlap, but again the purpose is not to administer a sophisticated personality inventory but rather set up the conditions under which specific personality factors can be observed and assessed in a practical manner.

The use of the Children's Personality Questionnaire (CPQ) and the 16 Personality Factors for Adolescents (16PF) can then support and add to this information. It can provide objective reinforcement of information gained from the questionnaires, or it may raise questions that must then be further explored.

PERSONALITY FACTORS

In the preceding discussion it was pointed out that a definition of personality is difficult due to the number of theoretical viewpoints held by various professionals concerning personality structure. On one end of the continuum there is the strictly psychodynamic orientation, which relies on a large number of integrated concepts concerning unconscious and sociocultural factors, which are extremely variable from theorist to theorist. Conversely, the opposing viewpoint is that of the behaviorist, who relies on a range of theories related to perceptual and behavioral factors primarily respondent to conditioning from the environment. The latter theory appears to suggest that personality is formed by and is primarily a function of environmental opportunity, reinforcement, and shaping toward certain desired behaviors. Between these two theories are a number of others, which tend to integrate the two somewhat or take a more philosophical-religious orientation such as humanistic concepts.

For the practicing mental health professional who is not a psychologist, application or even understanding of many of these theories requires more subtle discrimination of personality factors and professional training than is or has been available to the individual. However, this individual needs some sort of personality instrument that can provide information that is consistent with interviews and analysis of on-the-spot behaviors of the child at home and school. The preceding factors in temperament and locus of control provide a good range of person-to-person sampling of the child's general personality.

Earlier in our discussion a test series was mentioned that provides this objective analysis in association with the interview format presented in the earlier part of the chapter. The Children's Personality Questionnaire is an objective instrument, which can add information to the interview analysis and at the same time substantiate much of what is gained through the interviews. There are other forms of The Children's Personality Questionnaire that include questionnaires for young children, ages six to eight, called The Early School Personality Questionnaire (ESPQ), and one for high school students called The High School Personality Questionnaire (HSPQ). These tests provide a range of information concerning personality factors, which is quite helpful to psychologists and counselors. The tests are primarily designed for interpretation by psychologists and counselors, but in clinical situations a social worker, teacher, or behavioral clinician is able to administer the tests and provide interpretation under the supervision of the psychologist or counselor. Thus, without the need to use sophisticated projective instruments such as the Rorschach or the Minnesota Multiphasic Personality Inventory, the teacher, counselor, or clinician can use information of a more clinical nature.

The basic test in the personality questionnaire series is the 16 Personality Factors (16PF). The original test was designed to look at sixteen specific personality factors, which are designed upon a web of psychological theory and provide sixteen independent personality variables. The HSPQ, the ESPQ, and the CPQ are similar instruments for younger individuals.

The personality factors involved in the tests are presented below in a paraphrased form to assist the reader in understanding the basic nature of the tests.

1. Factor A — The first factor is an analysis of the individual's tendency toward either highly reserved or highly outgoing characteristics.

2. Factor B — The second factor samples behavior that relates concrete thinking processes to abstract thinking processes and presumes to identify the nature of the individual's cognitive style.

3. Factor C — The third factor involves analysis of the individual's tendencies toward high sensitivity and emotionality on one hand or toward high stable and mature emotional orientation on the other hand.

4. Factor D — This factor involves a comparison of tendencies toward inactive versus overactive behavior.

5. Factor E — In this factor the concern is with tendencies to be obedient and accommodating as opposed to being assertive and aggressive.

6. Factor F — In this factor the extremes of seriousness and enthusiasm are considered.

7. Factor G — Factor G compares tendencies toward expediency and conscientiousness.

8. Factor H — This factor compares tendencies toward being shy or being adventurous.

9. Factor I — This factor compares tendencies toward rejection of illusions and tough mindedness to sensitivity and overprotectedness.

10. Factor J — This factor compares interest in group action and successfulness to reflectiveness and restraint.

11. Factor O — This factor compares self-assuredness to apprehensiveness.

12. Factor Q2 —This factor compares social dependence to self-sufficiency.

13. Factor Q3 —This factor compares impulsiveness to self-discipline.

14. Factor Q4 —Emotional states of relaxed to tense are analyzed in this final factor.

These factors provide an extensive analysis of the individual's personality functioning in these dimensions. Obviously, skill in interpretation is required for understanding this test. However, teachers, behavioral clinicians, and other professionals can administer and score the test and with assistance from the staff or organization psychologist or counselor are able to apply the data. In cases where complex personality problems exist, the professional will usually consult with or be supervised by a psychologist. For school settings where the teacher may wish to use her own skills such as with the questions at the beginning of the chapter, use of this test would not be needed. Intervention could occur on only the interview forms already presented. In some cases, the teacher could administer the personality factors test and gain additional information and verification of her own interpretation. This is an effective use of the psychologist's time.

This chapter provides the personality survey required for the total developmental overview of the child's behavior. If only personality were to be assessed, then a much more extensive screening would be needed. When personality is screened along with the many other factors already mentioned, much personality data will have been gathered from the first three sections of the book. To this point the professional will have looked at language intelligence, perceptual-motor function, school achievement, and finally personality. These areas will yield much information even though total time in assessment will be minimal. In the last chapter we will look at the final area, social development.

Chapter 8

SOCIAL BEHAVIORAL ASSESSMENTS

A SSESSMENT OF A CHILD'S general social behavior is difficult
for the diagnostician in a clinical setting, but many other
mental health workers including the teacher will have access to
observation of this sort of behavior. What the teacher can accomplish through observation the clinic staff can accomplish
through interview, testing, and communications with the school.
Thus far the comprehensive evaluation has included
perceptual-motor development, school achievement, language
and intellectual development, and personality. Social development in a very real sense is the culmination of the behavioral
competencies of the child in other areas. It might be assumed
that if the child is competent in the other areas of development
then this one should take care of itself. Interestingly, this is not
necessarily the case; rather, the social area of development is one
in which there is a great deal of variability between children. It is
also one that, though we often refer to it as an important aspect
of school and community behavior, is not very well taught or
given to practice within the school setting. Somehow it seems that
adults teach certain rules to a child, reinforce them with rewards
or punishment, and then somehow expect that the child will put
it all together. The result is a population of adults who are largely
socially incompetent. That we grow up and adjust somehow in
the great stream of society is more or less a miracle.

What is social behavior? What is it that a child is supposed to
learn but does not that subsequently creates problems for him?
Social behavior involves two great issues in the human drama —
learning to obtain one's own personal needs from others, and
learning how to communicate and participate in interpersonal
relationships to achieve maintenance of one's family and community responsibilities. These two major areas of social behavior
encompass nearly all of what are commonly referred to as social
skills. There must be specific areas of behavior developed from
these global concepts.

136

PERSONAL NEED-SERVING BEHAVIOR

A mother's love is purported to be unselfish and complete for her children. It is not. An infant grows into a child and the task of childhood is to become an independent human being separate from the mother's security and all-pervasive direction. This is one of the great dilemmas for both the child and the mother. It is one of the most important human dramas. If it works successfully, capable and independent humans develop from helpless infants. If it works poorly, maladaptive and dependent adults emerge. It works as often in one direction as in the other. That is the *why* for this book.

One of the great tasks of socialization is that of learning to organize one's behavior in such a way as to gain acceptance from others and also to get personal needs served. Children come to school with varying degrees of social abilities, and often there is not an adequate amount of attention within the curriculum given to helping children to develop social skills. Socialization is far more complex than merely playing with other children, taking your turn, and sharing toys. Social skills are the means by which the child learns to obtain affection, recognition, cooperation, and even social status from others. Typical of the social skills required by the school would be the following:

1. Cooperation
2. Sharing with others
3. Giving respect to others
4. Obeying school and classroom rules
5. Completing work assignments
6. Being courteous to others
7. Helping others

There are many other skills, but these are good examples. From the standpoint of the child, though, what are the basic *personal* skills that make it possible for one to demonstrate the above skills? That is what the teacher and mental health worker must examine with the parents. How are social skills built, and what may be the problems when a child is not able to learn or act in appropriate ways toward others?

The following factors appear to be important in forming social skills. Each one can be observed by parents and teachers; for the most part, these factors can be taught, to assure that the child is able to develop effective social skills.

REALISTIC AND EFFECTIVE SELF-CONCEPT

It can be recognized that the child who has a positive self-concept will more likely be able to organize effectively his behavior with others. How does the child see himself? If he displays a self-concept, as discussed in the preceding chapter, that has major deficits, then those areas will need attention prior to the development of the effective social skills.

ACCEPTANCE OF PERSONAL RESPONSIBILITY

Also mentioned in the last chapter was the issue of personal locus of control and subsequent personal responsibility. Personal responsibility implies that the child accepts that he must act in certain ways to obtain the responses that he desires from the environment. In the preceding chapter this area was reviewed through the use of a questionnaire. That questionnaire and the responses should be reviewed as part of the social evaluation.

Specific social factors that may be evaluated include the following. These should be assessed with the foregoing major areas of personal responsibility and self-concept clearly in mind.

1. *Recognition of the needs of others*
   Does the child recognize and respond to the needs of others? The young child has difficulty recognizing the needs of others because he expects others to be concerned about him. He is egocentric and unable to direct his perception away from himself. As he becomes more self-controlled and participatory in social behavior, the child learns to recognize the needs of others. This is not always an easy task and one that takes much assistance from adults. Once a child does learn to recognize the needs of others he is not only able to assist in social groups, he learns that by serving the needs of others his own also get served. Manipulative children learn this principle early and tend to attempt to give others what they want so as to get positive feedback from others.

There are many reasons why a child may not attend to the needs of others or be able to effectively respond in ways that reinforce others. The child with an egocentric personality structure is a child who generally feels unworthy, who has feelings of anger toward adults. He has dominant, aggressive tendencies, and withdrawal or fearful feelings. The basis for poor social recognition of the needs of others must be explored through interview and questioning of both the child and the parent.

2. *Internalization of social values*

Through the guidance, reinforcement, and authority of the parents, the young child accepts limitations on his behavior in the form of behavioral rules. As the child matures he accepts these rules, internalizes them, and acts upon them as his own. This process of first responding and submitting to the external rules of parents and adults and then internalizing rules is a critical process in social maturation. The rules, in reality, are usually more than just rules, they are social values. The child goes through many stages of moral or social-value development. Our interest here is only in a few of them. These are

a. The good boy-bad boy stage;

b. The cops and robbers stage;

c. The democratic stage.

Young children arrive at what might be called the good boy-bad boy stage of moral development somewhere between the ages of five to seven years. At this stage the child has internalized values only to the degree that he models and repeats the "black and white" rules and values he has heard. He acts appropriately because being good brings rewards and being bad brings punishment. He does not evaluate the rules but merely models them to avoid punishment and gain reward.

This initial stage of internalizing values provides for the child an internal reference for his behavior, and he is likely to state that he is a good boy because he does such and such without really knowing any subtle or personal reason for doing so. This stage of development provides a stability for the child in learning to practice appropriate behaviors. As the child behaves in the appropriate way he not only develops a personal self-concept of being a "good boy" but also practices behaviors that will become cemented into appropriate social skills. Some of the values that are in the process of being internalized include the following at this stage:

1. Good boys do what adults tell them to do.
2. Good boys go to school and learn.
3. Good boys tell the truth.
4. Good boys do not hurt other children.
5. Good boys say "please," "I'm sorry," and ask for permission.
6. Good boys do their part, show aggression, like to compete, and are winners.

These are but a few of the values that are communicated to the boys. Some of these hold true for girls, but there are additional values for girls that are no less difficult. The reader can easily guess what these might be. It is important to understand that the teaching of these values and the child's acceptance of them is a significant milestone in the child's social development, for it is upon these values that he will base his future social behavior. Some children do not learn these values, and it is somewhat easy to guess how this might happen. The following problems often precipitate a lack of good value learning:

1. A lack of parental supervision and training.
2. Conflicting messages from parents concerning values — the parents disagree or behave inconsistently themselves relative to what they tell the children.
3. Poor models of adult behavior in the home.
4. Parents who are overly permissive and do not reinforce or communicate clearly defined rules.
5. Parents who are uncomfortable with authority themselves or who are rebellious toward authority.
6. Parents who are overly democratic or who are overindulgent with their children.

The mental health professional will have to investigate both with the parents and children the nature of the home environment in these areas.

The second stage of value development includes children from eight to thirteen years of age and might be labeled the legalistic or cops and robbers stage. At this level the child not only becomes aware of the rules but has internalized them both emotionally and intellectually. Children at this age like stories where the good guys win, and we give them much of these both at school and on television. At this age the child is very conscious of "fairness" and doing the right thing. Children may sometimes even begin to criticize their parents or teacher when they do something that the child feels is wrong.

Heroes become important at this age, and the child is now forming in his mind a growing personal belief system that fits into the ideal of the culture. There is another growing internal awareness in the child that will erupt sometime in adolescence, causing a major crisis for the child. The child, while he is very moralistic and conscious of fairness, is also being caught more and more in situations where things are not right or wrong but somewhere in between. At first this does not create much of a problem, but by the time the child enters adolescence it becomes a real issue. As the child enters adolescence not only is his thinking becoming more complex but so is his need to be accepted as an adult and allowed to make more personal decisions. It all centers on gaining personal freedom, the first stage of leaving the cocoon, and the eventual establishment of independence from home and parents.

As the child enters adolescence his thinking becomes more and more critical of the general value system of adults. He begins to see things are seldom "black or white" and he has to learn to assess behavior from a situational viewpoint rather than from a right-wrong dichotomy. Finally he arrives at an independent viewpoint of right and wrong, which can fit into the many discrepancies of real life.

In assessing a child's development socially, the foregoing factors must be taken into account. The child who has internalized very few values will have difficulty determining the appropriateness of his behavior, and certainly this lack of social framework will create problems in social behavior.

3. Interpersonal Communications

Interpersonal communication is simply talking or nonverbally communicating to another person. This is a simple concept that is the essence of social relationships and of substance in the complex issues of human behavior. How, why, when, and if the child communicates is of great importance in assessing his overall behavioral competencies. It is of some significance that even while we, the evaluators, attempt to understand the communication skills of the child too often we do little better in our own communications. That should be kept in mind as we attempt to place judgments on a child's ability to communicate to others.

In assessing the child's communication and interpersonal relationships we must take care not to place too much emphasis on how well or how poorly the child fares, for it is very difficult to assess. Each child has his own uniqueness involving what is or is not appropriate for him. For example, we often find that parents of highly gifted children, particularly creative gifted children, worry about the lack of good interpersonal relationships and communication that seems to exist between their child and their child's friends. A most frequent concern in fact is that their child does not have any friends. This is often borne out in that the child may have one friend but seldom several, and he and his friend spend their time making or creating things but do not engage in the normal social relationships of their peer group.

The highly gifted child often finds friends on the basis of mutual interests and not for social reasons. This seems odd to other children and to the parents, for they do not understand that these children are different even if they like to think they are not. Then, there is the quiet child who prefers his world of fantasy, music, making things, or just playing alone. He seems happy, but the parents worry about him just the same. Who is to say that his happiness is any less appropriate than the child who is highly competitive and social?

It is more important to know how the child feels about personal relationships than how adults feel. It is only when the child has difficulties in interpersonal relationships, when he *wants* friends that he does not have, that we should be concerned. It is important to intervene in a child's world when he attempts interpersonal relationships and fails, when he is abusive to others, when he disrupts, or when he develops deviant forms of social interaction. We must be very careful with our assessment of a child's social relationships. The authors once asked a child why he did not talk more in school and with his peers, and he replied, "Because I have nothing to say." That ended the evaluation.

It is important, within the total assessment, to attempt to understand the child's social behavior and then determine if intervention is needed. The teacher and parents should, however, be given specific areas rather than vague statements about the child's needs. Exactly what is it that everyone should be concerned with and attempt to alter?

There are few tests or instruments that are effective in assessing interpersonal relationships or skills. For this reason the authors usually attempt to make assessment of these skills through parent or child interviews followed by information gained from the school. Three global areas mentioned here, recognition of needs of others, internalization of social values, and interpersonal communication, provide a general framework of looking at social behavior. These are not the only areas of concern in social behavior, but they provide critical aspects of this area that have not been covered elsewhere in the total assessment. The following questionnaire can be given to both the parents and the child. A copy can be forwarded to the teacher at school, where it will reflect actual observations of behavior. The areas listed provide a somewhat comprehensive range of social behaviors.

Social Recognition Skills

1. *Rights of others* — Awareness and acceptance of the rights of other people as distinct from the child's.

   a. Does your child respect the ownership of toys and objects by others? Does he ask permission to play with them rather than merely taking them?   1 2 3 4 5 6 7 8 9 10

   b. Does your child accept and abide by
     the rules at school and home de-
     signed for group management?   1 2 3 4 5 6 7 8 9 10

2. *Identification* — A feeling of being like others, of being one of a particular group, of having an identification with a particular group.

   a. Does your child display awareness
     and pride in belonging to a particular
     classroom, sports team, or organized
     group?   1 2 3 4 5 6 7 8 9 10

   b. Does your child reflect attitudes and
     feelings of a special group to which
     he belongs?   1 2 3 4 5 6 7 8 9 10

3. *Participation* — Actively seeking membership in special groups and joining their activity such as scouts, sports teams, or other groups.

   a. Does your child display interest in
     and request an opportunity to belong
     to a group?   1 2 3 4 5 6 7 8 9 10

   b. Is your child able to play or work with
     others in a group independently
     without being distracted by the
     group?   1 2 3 4 5 6 7 8 9 10

4. *Cooperation* — Working with others in a cooperative way to accomplish a task that could not be accomplished alone.

   a. Does your child seek assistance from
     others to work on a project or to play
     a game?   1 2 3 4 5 6 7 8 9 10

   b. Does your child display willingness
     and ability to play with others in a
     group or team activity that requires
     cooperation or teamwork?   1 2 3 4 5 6 7 8 9 10

5. *Competition* — To enjoy and seek opportunities to play or work "against" others toward individual or group "winning."

   a. Does your child display an interest in
     maintaining behavior in a competi-
     tive situation with a positive attitude?   1 2 3 4 5 6 7 8 9 10

b. Does your child appear motivated to
achieve and win in competitive situations? 1 2 3 4 5 6 7 8 9 10

6. *Leadership* — The interest in and willingness to accept responsibility for making decisions that affect and direct the
behavior of others.

a. Does your child actively seek status
with other children so as to have
control and dominance in play and
work situations? 1 2 3 4 5 6 7 8 9 10

b. Does your child feel comfortable in
accepting personal responsibility for
the behavior of a group? 1 2 3 4 5 6 7 8 9 10

7. *Trustworthiness* — The skill of being reliable, of accepting
personal responsibility for behavior toward others, of giving
a feeling of confidence to others.

a. Does your child display attitudes of
concern and responsibility for
others, for being trustworthy with
others? 1 2 3 4 5 6 7 8 9 10

b. Does your child have esteem for
others? Does he seek recognition for
being dependable from others? 1 2 3 4 5 6 7 8 9 10

8. *Friendship* — The general behavioral expression of positive
acceptance and feeling toward others.

a. Does your child display positive
feelings toward others — smiling,
hugging, saying positive things? 1 2 3 4 5 6 7 8 9 10

b. Does your child display loyalty toward others and feelings of respon-
sibility for the welfare of others? 1 2 3 4 5 6 7 8 9 10

9. *Helpfulness* — The act of assisting others, of giving aid and
support to their needs.

a. Does your child display spontaneous
acts of giving things or assistance to
others? 1 2 3 4 5 6 7 8 9 10

b. Does your child show concern for the
ability of others, for helping them

learn to do something or improve
themselves?   1 2 3 4 5 6 7 8 9 10

10. *Empathy* — The awareness of the feelings of others and a
willingness to attempt to understand their needs.
   a. Does your child display appropriate
      concern and feelings of under-
      standing toward situations and
      events that affect others?   1 2 3 4 5 6 7 8 9 10
   b. Does your child feel the happiness
      and pain of others with true empathy
      followed by comforting behaviors?   1 2 3 4 5 6 7 8 9 10

Social Values

11. *Right-wrong Concepts* — The awareness and internalization
of a belief system relative to the appropriateness or inap-
propriateness of behavior.
   a. Does your child display an awareness
      of right and wrong behaviors and re-
      spond to misbehavior with appropri-
      ate feelings of remorse and guilt?   1 2 3 4 5 6 7 8 9 10
   b. Does your child tend to make judg-
      ments of others on the basis of a con-
      sistent set of rules or beliefs?   1 2 3 4 5 6 7 8 9 10

12. *Internalization* — The process of accepting social values as
one's own and acting on those values.
   a. Does your child appear to accept the
      values code he espouses as his own
      rather than merely saying what he
      has heard is correct and acceptable? 1 2 3 4 5 6 7 8 9 10
   b. Is the child's rule system consistent
      with that of the parents' or school's as
      opposed to developing a rule system
      that is in opposition to others?   1 2 3 4 5 6 7 8 9 10

13. *Alteration of Values* — The act of developing some personal
alteration in the value system taught to the child.
   a. Does your child display some dis-
      agreement with certain values or be-
      liefs but in a positive way? Does he
      tend to act on his own, slightly al-
      tered, values in a consistent manner? 1 2 3 4 5 6 7 8 9 10

b. Does your child display the ability to objectively assess new values that are being espoused by a peer group, an authority figure, or family member, and accept or reject them on the basis of personal good?   1 2 3 4 5 6 7 8 9 10

14. *Value Objectivity* — The ability to evaluate one's values or the values of the group without personal bias.

a. Is your child able to recognize and understand values of others without attempting to inflict his beliefs on them?   1 2 3 4 5 6 7 8 9 10

b. Can your child play with and interact with others who display different belief systems? Can he work out a compromise with such individuals that allows for positive social interaction?   1 2 3 4 5 6 7 8 9 10

15. *Value Constancy* — The ability to structure one's behavior in different situations in ways that provide a consistency of adherence to one's basic values.

a. Does your child tend to behave in ways that suggest his values consistently affect his behavior?   1 2 3 4 5 6 7 8 9 10

b. Do the child's behaviors indicate that he is clearly aware of values he holds and do such values inhibit his behavior appropriately?   1 2 3 4 5 6 7 8 9 10

16. *Approach-Withdrawal* — Displaying approach behaviors to others, or having a tendency to withdraw from social interaction.

a. Does your child seem to enjoy meeting new children?   1 2 3 4 5 6 7 8 9 10

b. Does your child take the initiative in new situations to become acquainted with others?   1 2 3 4 5 6 7 8 9 10

17. *Expressiveness* — The willingness and ability to express one's feelings and ideas to others.

a. Does your child tell others how he feels and share his ideas with them? 1 2 3 4 5 6 7 8 9 10

  b. Does your child attempt to interject
     his ideas into group discussions, and
     does he display feelings of assertive-
     ness in situations where others chal-
     lenge his ideas?   1 2 3 4 5 6 7 8 9 10
18. *Listening Skills* — The willingness of an individual to listen to
    others in an understanding way.
  a. Does your child like to listen to others
     without attempting to dominate the
     conversation?   1 2 3 4 5 6 7 8 9 10
  b. Does your child appear to be able to
     listen to others and attempt to under-
     stand their viewpoint? Is he sup-
     portive of others?   1 2 3 4 5 6 7 8 9 10
19. *Assertiveness* — The willingness and action of asserting one's
    own beliefs and role.
  a. Does your child display personal as-
     sertiveness with others that estab-
     lishes him as an individual rather
     than merely a follower?   1 2 3 4 5 6 7 8 9 10
  b. Does your child state his beliefs and
     expectations, or does he merely ac-
     cept the interest of others without
     attempting to follow his own inter-
     ests?   1 2 3 4 5 6 7 8 9 10
20. *Inquisitiveness* — The intentional inquiring of others for
    information, ideas, and knowledge.
  a. Does your child show curiosity about
     the ideas others have?   1 2 3 4 5 6 7 8 9 10
  b. Does your child display an inquiring
     mind that desires new information to
     be used, and then alter his behavior
     in some way?   1 2 3 4 5 6 7 8 9 10
21. *Directedness* — The intentional behavior of an individual that
    displays personal volition toward change.
  a. Does your child display behavior that
     suggests an achievement drive, to
     learn and to change both himself
     and/or his environment?   1 2 3 4 5 6 7 8 9 10

b. Is your child's behavior purposeful at
least from his viewpoint?   1 2 3 4 5 6 7 8 9 10

22. *Nurturance* — Displaying a need to help others, to give to
others, and to add positively to the welfare of the group.
   a. Does your child display affectionate
   behavior with other children or
   adults? Does he appear to want to
   please others?   1 2 3 4 5 6 7 8 9 10
   b. Does your child appear to enjoy
   doing things that make others happy
   without the apparent need for some
   sort of personal gain?   1 2 3 4 5 6 7 8 9 10

23. *Altruism* — The child displays the willingness and ability to
do for others in situations that may be detrimental to himself.
   a. Is your child able or willing to sac-
   rifice his own needs for the good of
   someone else or to increase group or
   individual gain?   1 2 3 4 5 6 7 8 9 10
   b. Is your child willing, in certain situations, to allow others some sort of
   gain even though it may become a
   loss to him?   1 2 3 4 5 6 7 8 9 10

24. *Sense of Community* — The child displays a sense of belonging
and accepting responsibility within the group.
   a. Does your child feel pleased when he
   is able to accept a role within a group
   that inhances the group?   1 2 3 4 5 6 7 8 9 10
   b. Does your child accept responsibility
   for a role of leadership in accom-
   plishing a group goal?   1 2 3 4 5 6 7 8 9 10

25. *Affiliation* — The child enjoys being around a group of
people. He enjoys belonging to a group and sharing with
them.
   a. Does your child seek out other
   playmates or friends to share time
   with?   1 2 3 4 5 6 7 8 9 10

    b. Does your child plan activities that
will include several others rather
than just one friend?   1 2 3 4 5 6 7 8 9 10

These twenty-five specific areas of social abilities are seldom recognized in formal evaluations and socialization. There are many other areas that could be mentioned, but this list will provide an extensive amount of information for the mental health professional concerning a child's socialization behavior. The checklist is an informal but structured way of looking at behavior. Further these areas are observable and can form a basis for action in changing the child's behavior. These skills can be taught to children in the classroom, at home, and in the clinic. They can provide behavior objectives in determining exactly what the adults should focus on during intervention activities. Scoring the profile, as in much of the information in this book, is less important than gaining recognition of specific areas of need for a particular child. The framework of this book is to assist mental health professionals in looking at specific behaviors across the broad range of human abilities. Much of what has been presented here can be understood and used by both professionals and parents. This sort of comprehensive assessment can provide definite areas of action for the mental health professional without the need for a complete psychological evaluation. If additional testing and assessment are required, the information here will be a valuable aid to both the mental health professional and the psychologist.

Further Readings

1. Hersh, R. J., Paolitto, D. P. and Reimer, J. R.: *Promoting Moral Growth.* New York, Longman, 1979.
2. Cohn, Stewart: *Social and Personality Development in Childhood.* New York, Macmillan, 1976.

INDEX

151

words spelled phonetically but incor-
rectly, 107
Spradlin, W. W., 26
Standing on one foot, 67
State institutions, 42
Stimulants, 30
Strategies in psychometric services, 9
Symbols, comprehension of, 10

T

Teachers, vi
Team-based diagnosis, v
Temperament, 117-121
  activity level, 118-119
  adaptability, 118, 120
  approach-withdrawal, 118, 120
  attention span, 118, 120
  checklist, 119-121
  distractibility, 118, 120
  environment in relation to, 121
  factors in, 118
  importance of, 121
  intensity of reaction, 118, 120
  persistence, 118, 120
  personality differentiated from, 118
  personal responsibility, 122, 124-125
  quality of mood, 118, 121
  rhythmicity, 118-120
  self-modulation, 118, 121
  threshold of responsiveness, 118, 121
Temper tantrums, 115
Thomas, A., 118 fnt.
Threshold of responsiveness, 118, 121
Traditional schools, 40
Trustworthiness, 145

U

Underachievement, 103
Ungraded schools, 38
Unrealistic expectations of parents, 25

V

Verbal expressive ability, 59-60
Verbal expressive disorders, 7
Verbal functions, 17
Verbal skills, 7, 9
Verbal-to-motor function, 69
Vision problems, 74
Vision screening, 9-10
Vision tests, 74
Visual deficits, 22, 98
Visual fixation difficulties, 98-99
Visualization of objects, 18
Visual-motor coordination, 65-66
Visual perception development, 59
Visual-perceptual screening, 9-10
Visual-perceptual skills, 7
Visual pursuit, 70
Visual skills, 70-74
Visual-to-motor function, 69
Visual tracking difficulties, 98-99
Visually handicapped children, 42

W

Wechsler Adult Intelligence Scale (WAIS),
  16-17
Wechsler Intelligence Scale for Children
  (WISC), 16-18, 23-24
  intellectual factors involved in subtests,
    20
  performance subtests, 19
  verbal subtests, 17-18
Wechsler Preschool and Primary Scale of
  Intelligence (WPPSI), 16-17, 23
Wide Range Achievement Test (WRAT),
  96-97, 99, 103, 105, 113
Withdrawn children, 83-84
Word recognition, 7, 97-98, 103
Writing, efficiency in, 104
Writing skills, 7, 103-105

Z

Zimmerman Preschool Language Scale,
  46-47, 60